ROUTLEDGE LIBRARY EDITIONS:
WORK & SOCIETY

Volume 13

LOCAL PARTNERSHIP & THE UNEMPLOYMENT CRISIS IN BRITAIN

LOCAL PARTNERSHIP &
THE UNEMPLOYMENT CRISIS
IN BRITAIN

CHRIS MOORE
AND
J. J. RICHARDSON

in association with
JEREMY MOON

Routledge
Taylor & Francis Group

LONDON AND NEW YORK

First published in 1989 by Unwin Hyman Ltd

This edition first published in 2024
by Routledge
4 Park Square, Milton Park, Abingdon, Oxon OX14 4RN

and by Routledge
605 Third Avenue, New York, NY 10158

Routledge is an imprint of the Taylor & Francis Group, an informa business

British Library Cataloguing in Publication Data
A catalogue record for this book is available from the British Library

ISBN: 978-1-032-80236-7 (Set)
ISBN: 978-1-032-81478-0 (Volume 13) (hbk)
ISBN: 978-1-032-81486-5 (Volume 13) (pbk)
ISBN: 978-1-003-50010-0 (Volume 13) (ebk)

DOI: 10.4324/9781003500100

Publisher's Note
The publisher has gone to great lengths to ensure the quality of this reprint but points out that some imperfections in the original copies may be apparent.

Disclaimer
The publisher has made every effort to trace copyright holders and would welcome correspondence from those they have been unable to trace.

Local partnership and the unemployment crisis in Britain

CHRIS MOORE and J. J. RICHARDSON
(University of Strathclyde)

in association with
JEREMY MOON
(University of Western Australia)

London
UNWIN HYMAN
Boston   Sydney   Wellington

Published by the Academic Division of

Unwin Hyman Ltd
15/17 Broadwick Street, London W1V 1FP, UK

Unwin Hyman Inc.,
8 Winchester Place, Winchester, Mass. 01890, USA

Allen & Unwin (Australia) Ltd,
8 Napier Street, North Sydney, NSW 2060, Australia

Allen & Unwin (New Zealand) Ltd in association with the
Port Nicholson Press Ltd,
Compusales Building, 75 Ghuznee Street, Wellington 1, New Zealand

First published in 1989

British Library Cataloguing in Publication Data

Moore, Chris
    Local partnership and the unemployment crisis in Britain.
    (New local government series).
    1. Great Britain. Unemployment. Regional variations.
    I. Title II. Richardson, J. J. (Jeremy John) III. Moon, Jeremy 1955–
    IV. Series
    331.13′7941
ISBN 0-04-352220-3

Library of Congress Cataloging-in-Publication Data

Moore, Chris, B. A.
    Local partnership and the unemployment crisis in Britain/by Chris
    Moore and J. J. Richardson, in association with Jeremy Moon.
    p. cm.
    Bibliography: p.
    Includes index.
    ISBN 0-04-352220-3.
    1. Industrial promotion—Great Britain. 2. Partnership—Great Britain.
    3. Unemployment—Great Britain. 4. Great Britain—Full employment
    policies.
    I. Richardson, J. J. (Jeremy John). II. Moon, Jeremy, 1955–. III. Title.
    HC260.I53M66 1989   89-9030
    331.13′7941—dc20   CIP

Typeset in 10 on 12 point Bembo by Fotographics (Bedford) Ltd

Contents

Preface

The issue of historically high levels of unemployment and of the most appropriate policy responses to it has emerged as one of high political salience. Within the myriad of policy responses at supranational, national, regional and local levels we have seen a rapid growth of a new form of public–private partnership variously termed the local enterprise trust or local enterprise agency (LEA).

While considerable attention has been paid to public-sector responses to local economic decline, there has been relatively little *critical* analysis of the workings of this local partnership model. The proponents of corporate involvement in local economic regeneration initiatives in association with the public sector have been keen to claim the success of such collaborative ventures. However, it is an opportune moment for an outside assessment of what has been happening at the local level, through these new agencies which have been set up to combat unemployment and to stimulate growth.

This book aims to analyse the responses to unemployment in terms of the policy process and institutional arrangements operating at the local level, and how these interact with other levels of the policy network. However, we are also concerned to assess the impacts of these new responses on the economic welfare of their local communities.

Drawing on the authors' own past and current research into various aspects of unemployment and local economic policy, as well as on secondary materials, the book assesses critically the contribution of local enterprise agencies and how this relates to other dimensions of the policy responses to unemployment. An important element of the analysis is a number of local case studies of established partnership in different parts of the UK: namely, Neath, Dumbarton, Tyne and Wear and St Helens. By offering a comparative analysis based on selected studies, complemented by wider research findings, the book hopes to contribute to an understanding of the factors involved in making effective responses through this type of mechanism, in terms of organizational structures and networks and programmes of activity. Thus, we go beyond descriptions of a series of individual initiatives, towards a broader analysis of policy processes and policy impacts, linking specific cases with an overview of the key issues involved.

Given the critical importance of the unemployment issue for policy-makers and for the wider community, we hope that our study provides an informed and critical but non-technical analysis of the rapidly growing local responses to the unemployment problem.

The structure of the book is as follows. Chapter 1 provides a general review of the unemployment problem in the UK, analysing the nature of the crisis in the context of the economy as a whole, and suggests a broad characterization of the responses made at national level. Chapter 2 discusses how the problem affects local economies and communities and examines competing responses at this level. Chapter 3 looks in more detail at the organizational dynamics of local response through public–private partnership, drawing extensively on our original research of several enterprise agencies. The focus in this chapter is on relationships between the public and private sectors. Chapter 4 turns the analysis to an assessment of local policies and programmes offered by these agencies. Chapter 5 provides a more general evaluation of local responses and discusses how impacts can be measured. Finally, Chapter 6 attempts an interpretation of these developments in a broader political and ideological context, with special emphasis on the nature and meaning of private-sector involvement.

We would like to acknowledge the extensive help we received from all of the enterprise agencies we visited during our study. The book draws on data gathered from personal interviews with project managers and staff, sponsors from the public and private sectors and government officials at regional level. In addition, we enjoyed access to the records and background reports of the various enterprise agencies.

We would particularly like to express our special thanks to the Neath Development Partnership, which formed the central core study. The Partnership officials and their colleagues in Neath Borough Council were generous with their time and patient with our questioning. We also wish to express an equal debt of gratitude to the International Thomson Organization, one of Neath's founder sponsors, for funding the study. We should make clear that ITO is in no way responsible for the conclusions or views presented here and we are especially grateful to them for allowing us total freedom in carrying out critical analysis and research without trying to influence the outcome. We hope in return we have made some pertinent contribution to the debate on enterprise agencies in the UK.

We would also like to thank Jeremy Moon for his valuable contribution to the project before his departure to Australia. He was responsible for getting the project off the ground and for initial research and has made comments on the draft. In addition we would like to thank Grace Hunter, Alison Robinson, Pat McTaggart and Anita Sansom for typing various stages of the research findings and the book. We are grateful to Unwin Hyman for their understanding and forbearance in waiting for delivery of the book.

Finally we should add the usual cautionary note by saying that we are responsible for any errors and omissions and for the views expressed.

Jeremy Richardson and
Chris Moore, Glasgow, February 1989

1 The politics of unemployment: the national context

The changing nature and perceptions of the unemployment problem

The decade 1978–88 has seen a major transformation in both the reality and the perceptions of the unemployment problem in Britain. Had this book been written even three years ago, we would have been totally pessimistic about the long-term future of the unemployed and for many of those fortunate to be still in work. Instead, official figures show that the unemployment level is at its lowest since 1981, at under 2.3 million (August 1988), down from a peak of approximately 3.3 million in September 1986, representing 8.1 per cent of the workforce, compared with 11.9 per cent of the workforce two years earlier (*Employment Gazette*, October 1988, p 518). Similarly, the trend in employment has been equally positive with over 1.6 million new jobs created in the economy since March 1983, with employment at the end of 1987 only 230,000 below the peak of December 1979 (*Labour Market Quarterly Report*, July 1988, p 2). Within this overall pattern, the changing balance of employment is very marked. During the 1980s, there has been a marked increase in the proportion of employment in self-employment, part-time employment, the service sector, and women employees. The decline in manufacturing and the rise of service sector employment is illustrated very clearly in Table 1.1, giving data for the period 1984–7.

The improving trend in both unemployment and employment is reflected in other indicators, too. For example, recruitment difficulties and skill shortages are now emerging, with 19 per cent of firms reporting expected skill shortages in April 1988, compared with approximately 3 per cent in 1982. (This phenomenon was not confined to Britain. The OECD's 1988 *Employment Report* published in September 1988, revealed a similar pattern in several European countries, with the emergence of labour shortages due to skills

Table 1.1   Change in employment, 1984–7 (thousands)

	Managerial and admin	Higher level service group	Higher level industrial group	Lower level service and supervisory group	Craft and foreman group	Lower level industrial and other group[a]	Total
Agriculture, forestry and fishing	−22.3	+1.5	+0.4	−0.7	+2.0	−16.6	−35.7
Energy and water supply	−9.8	−1.5	−7.2	−27.2	−46.4	−34.3	−126.4
Extr. mins, etc manuf. metals	−16.3	−2.1	−4.8	−6.2	+3.2	−37.3	−63.5
Metal goods, engineering, etc	−6.0	+25.3	+4.2	−16.3	−43.8	−28.3	−64.9
Other manuf. industries	−12.3	−0.4	+1.4	−10.5	+22.1	−34.5	−34.2
Construction	+1.6	+1.3	+26.7	+16.2	+19.9	−11.3	+54.4
Dist. hotels and repairs	+43.8	+19.4	+9.8	+121.2	+3.2	+33.4	+235.8
Transport, communications	+10.4	+17.7	−23.3	+3.9	+5.4	+50.9	+65.0
Banking, finance, etc.	+44.3	+134.2	+35.3	+163.6	+14.7	+36.3	+428.4
Other services	+141.8	+138.0	−10.6	+182.1	+30.5	+9.8	+491.6
No answers, etc.	−3.5	−8.3	−4.6	−16.6	−3.7	−50.1	−86.8
Total	+171.7	+325.1	+27.3	+409.5	+12.1	−82.0	+863.7

[a] Includes did not reply, etc.

Source: Department of Employment Labour Force Surveys.

mismatches.) A survey of 150 British companies conducted in 1988 revealed that 26 per cent of firms had substantially increased their recruitment of part-time staff during the previous year and that 50 per cent said they would increase recruitment of part-timers in the coming months. Employers, it was reported, 'were having to change their traditional workplace organization to accommodate women because of labour market pressures' (*Financial Times*, 30 September 1988). The labour market pressures referred to were due to a combination of an increasingly buoyant national economy (notwith-standing major regional variations – see below) and the anticipation of the long-term effects of the decline in 16–19-year-olds in the late 1980s and early 1990s. Thus, the number of 16–19-year-olds in work is expected to fall by 500,000 by 1995 because of demographic trends. Part-time workers accounted for 23 per cent of all employment in 1987, compared with 17 per cent in 1981. The author of one study of Britain's improved productivity has suggested that the improvement was in part due to the greater adaptability of the labour market by increased use of 'external workers': 'These workers are added to a company's main workforce but with inferior conditions of employment – allowing total labour costs to be more closely linked to market forces' (Kevin Boakes, reported in the *Financial Times*, 25 May 1988).

Even the supply bottlenecks of the stop-go era of the 1950s and 1960s had begun to appear by 1988. For example, British cement manufacturers, who in the depth of the recession were closing plants and making workers redundant, were having to import some supplies in order to meet a 16 per cent rise in orders during the first five months of 1988 compared with the equivalent periods in the previous year. Such problems were, no doubt, a reflection of a growth rate which exceeded 4 per cent in the second quarter of 1988 (following one of the best growth rates in Western Europe over the previous two or three years), as was the mounting trade deficit, predicted to be in excess of £10 billion by the end of 1988, as Britain's economy yet again sucked in imports in a period of rapid economic growth. (The economy has grown at an average of 3 per cent per year since 1981.) Not surprisingly, company profitability in the UK has risen rapidly from being one of the lowest in the OECD region to being one of the highest, with a corresponding increase in the share of output taken by profits, although the ratio of capital spending to corporate income has in fact declined since the 1970s. Although investment was reported to have increased very rapidly during 1988, surpassing the 1979 peak, the very high interest rates (introduced in order to dampen down what was thought to be an overheated economy), the rising balance of payments problems and the threat of rising inflation all combined to threaten the hard-won achievements of the previous few years.

That the achievements were indeed hard won was still very evident, even after several years of continuous economic growth, as the regional disparities remained as serious as ever. Thus, in August 1988 the unemployment rate in the South-East was 5.2 per cent; in East Anglia it was 4.7 per cent; in the West Midlands, 8.8 per cent; in Yorkshire and Humberside, 11.3 per cent; in the North-West, 13.1 per cent; in Wales, 10.4 per cent; in Scotland, 13.7 per cent, and in Northern Ireland, 20 per cent (*Employment Gazette*, October 1988). These variations in absolute levels of unemployment were paralleled by variations in the rate of decline in levels of unemployment. Thus, between August 1986 and September 1987 the fall in unemployment was 20.9 per cent in the South-East (excluding London), compared with 8.4 per cent in Scotland (*Labour Market Quarterly Report*, November 1987). The government's own publication *Regional Trends* also highlighted the gap in earnings between the North and

South of the country. Thus average weekly household income in the South-East was £269 in 1985–6, compared with £187 in the Northern region (*Regional Trends*, no. 23, 1988).

Changing reality or massaging indicators?

Behind the decline in the political salience of unemployment lay a debate over whether employment had *really* declined and whether the other positive indicators of economic success – such as improved productivity rates – were also somewhat illusory. The Labour Party's employment spokesman, Michael Meacher MP, claimed in September 1988 that much of the fall in unemployment was essentially the result of the government's nineteen 'statistical fiddles' and that the *real* level of unemployment was almost exactly 3 million (Meacher, 1988). Meacher argued that the Conservative government had, since 1979, been engaged in no less than nineteen statistical alterations in order artificially to lower the unemployment totals. For example, he cited the fact that in August 1988 all young people on the Youth Training Scheme (YTS) were counted as 'employed', whereas previously only 25 per cent of YTS trainees with contracts of employment were counted as employed. Thus, 'without creating a single extra job, the Government has bumped up the number of people classified as employed by 350,000 – and reduced the unemployment rate accordingly'. The government also stopped counting the number of unemployed school-leavers at all (in 1987 between 100,000 and 130,000 such youngsters were counted over the three summer months), and a further 106,000 under-18 unemployed people were excluded from the jobless total because they are no longer able to claim unemployment benefit. From September 1989 it is planned that all of the expected 600,000 on the new Employment Training Scheme (see below) will also be counted as 'employed'. On Meacher's calculation these measures have the effect of 'reducing' the number of unemployed by approximately 1 million, on top of sixteen other alleged 'fiddles', such as the decision in October 1982 to make it no longer compulsory for most of those receiving unemployment benefit to register at Job Centres. This, he claims, reduced the unemployment count by 190,000 or 6.2 per cent of the total.

Without necessarily accepting the full force of Mr Meacher's argument (he, after all, has as much political interest in *maximising* the unemployment count as the government does in *minimizing* it), it does illustrate the essentially *political* nature of the unemployment issue and the extent to which the issue is subject to a degree of game-playing by all but the unemployed themselves. Basically, we have no agreed definition or measure of unemployment. For example, the Employment Institute has calculated that if unemployment is measured by deducting the level of employment from the labour force, unemployment fell by 127,000 between March 1987 and March 1988, rather than by the official estimate of 504,000 (reported in the *Financial Times*, 16 June 1988). Changes in the 'rules of the game' can have quirkish effects, rendering debate about unemployment a rather surrealist pastime. For example, the Employment Institute has also noted that the numbers of long-term unemployed have fallen more rapidly than the total number of employed between 1987 and 1988 – a fact at variance with normal expectations. The reason, the Institute argues, is because unemployment benefits have become harder to get. Using such devices as 'summoning the long-term unemployed for a Restart interview, and by imposing a stricter availability-for-work test, the government has driven people off the unemployment register' (reported in *The Economist*, 28 May 1988).

Similar difficulties of interpreting results arise when we consider Britain's apparently good record on productivity since the early 1980s. Most observers have recognized the central importance of levels of productivity and rates of change in productivity in Britain, reflecting what is almost a conventional wisdom that historically low levels of productivity have been one of the major factors contributing to Britain's long-term decline (Gomulka, 1979; Brookings Institution, 1980). PA Consulting Group's survey of more than 800 companies in 1988 suggested that the impressive gains in productivity over the period 1984–8 had still left Britain lagging behind its competitors. On PA's calculations, if Britain's spectacular growth in productivity over the period 1983–7 (5.8 per cent, compared with 5.5 per cent in the USA, 5 per cent in Japan, 2.8 per cent in France and 2.6 per cent in West Germany) were to continue, it would still take Britain seven years to catch up with West Germany, eight years to catch up with France and more than twenty years to catch up with the USA, with Japan possibly far beyond reach (PA Consulting Group, 1988). Similar caution is expressed by Meen, who has calculated that between 1968 and 1973 the UK's 2.9 per cent growth in GDP left it behind most of its competitors apart from the USA; yet a very similar performance between 1981 and 1987 (gaining for Britain a new reputation as the dynamic economy of Western Europe rather than

Table 1.2   Comparative performance indicators, 1968–87

	GDP (1980 prices): average annual rate of growth			Labour productivity: average annual rate of growth			Unemployment rate: average		
	1968–73	1973–9	1979–87	1968–73	1973–9	1979–87	1968–73	1974–9	1980–7
UK	3.2	1.4	1.9	3.0	1.2	2.1	2.5	4.2	10.3
USA	3.0	2.6	2.3	0.7	0.0	0.6	4.7	6.8	7.7
Japan	8.4	3.6	3.9	7.3	2.9	2.9	1.2	1.9	2.5
W. Germany	4.9	2.3	1.5	4.1	2.9	1.5	0.8	3.5	6.9
France	6.2	2.8	1.7	5.0	2.5	1.8	2.6	4.7	9.0
Italy	4.6	2.6	2.3	4.6	1.8	1.7	5.4	6.2	9.1
Canada	5.4	4.2	2.8	2.4	1.3	1.0	5.4	7.2	9.8
Average	4.3	2.7	2.4	2.9	1.4	1.4	3.2	5.0	7.1

Source: OECD, 1987.

the 'sick man' of Europe) left Britain in only second place behind Japan (Meen, 1988). Essentially, Britian looked good because everyone else suddenly started doing as badly as Britain had traditionally been. Wolf's review of academic research on Britain's productivity record reveals the complexity of the debate and the difficulty in reaching agreed conclusions; although he argues that 'the productivity performance of the economy as a whole has unquestionably improved relative to that of the 1970s and of the country's peers', he also says that 'the deterioration of the performance of other industrial countries by comparison with the 1960s has been a much more important reason for the UK's relative success than improvements in the UK's own performance since then' (Wolf, 1988, reported in *Financial Times*, September 1988). Britain's comparative performance is illustrated by the OECD's calculations reproduced in Table 1.2, which show that although it had the worst unemployment record of seven selected countries (the UK, the USA, Japan, West Germany, France, Italy and Canada) the UK's average rate of growth in productivity was, as suggested above, high in comparative terms.

Fenstein's analysis also illustrates the turn-around in productivity growth in the UK over the period 1979–87. His analysis suggested that since 1979 Britain may have begun the very long process of catching up. The 'catch-up' process requires, he argues, awareness of the need for reform and for sustained exertion. His argument is that the recession of 1980–1 indeed helped to produce this awareness in Britain, supporting his theory that declining nations respond 'when the population at large has acquired the fundamental perception that *they* are now the relatively backward nation and must make every effort to reform their institutions and attitudes if they are not to sink progressively further behind' (Fenstein, 1989). It is not unreasonable to argue that unemployment policies – and indeed all other policies – were subservient to the Thatcher government's goal of re-enforcing this developing perception, so that fundamental attitudinal shifts could take place in society. Whether fundamental shifts in attitude have occurred remains to be seen. The 1988 edition of *British Social Attitudes* suggests that, if anything, support for an 'enterprise culture' has actually *dwindled* since 1979. Far from rejecting a 'dependency' culture, attitudes may have become 'less sympathetic to [the] central tenets of the Thatcher revolution' (Jowell, 1988).

Whether Britain's improvement – in terms of lowered unemployment, increased growth, or increased productivity – is 'real' or somewhat illusory, there is no denying that there has been much policy activity directed at affecting all three indicators of performance. Whether or not the big reductions in unemployment since 1986 have been by fiddling or massaging the statistics, the Conservative government has been very active in terms of policy innovation in generating anti-unemployment schemes, even though it was pursuing other more important goals. This book does not set out to review the range of national programmes, since our focus is on one specific aspect – *local* partnerships – of Britain's response to unemployment. However, before moving to our main concern in the subsequent chapters, it is perhaps useful to see if any broad trends in national policies can be discerned, as the context in which local partnership responses might be analysed.

Other objectives?

We should not overestimate the power of governments to change the world and to resist fundamental shifts in the balance of the world economy or in the nature of national economies. However, the Conservative government, first elected in 1979, has shown an unusual determination to pursue its own macro-economic and fiscal policies in a firmly held belief that this was the only way to secure a lasting economic recovery and a sustainable fall in the number of unemployed. In so far as it has been active in the field of unemployment policy (and it has in fact been very active), such policy is best seen as a means of managing an essentially political problem while the government's other overriding economic objectives were pursued (Richardson and Moon, 1984). These objectives have been many – from the early commitment to controlling the money supply and reducing public expenditure, to later and more sophisticated objectives of liberalizing the labour market, reducing the size of the old heavy industries and generally increasing the competitiveness of the business environment. To a considerable degree, all of these objectives were incompatible with short-term reductions in unemployment and, indeed, were more likely to *increase* the levels of unemployment. We see, therefore, the development of anti-unemployment policies as essentially a *political* response which, in the event, has proved enormously successful in its objective, namely, the avoidance of electoral defeat, notwithstanding mass (and for most of the period *rising*) unemployment. Even in early 1989 we need to remind ourselves that over 8 per cent of the working population (accepting the government's own disputed figures) is still out of work, with Britain now in its thirteenth year of unemployment above one million. The 'successful' political holding operation has enabled the government not only to pursue its other objectives (including major tax reforms designed to increase 'incentives') but also to bring about a major shift in the relative strengths and positions of the key actors in the 'unemployment industry' (Moon and Richardson, 1984a). Not only has unemployment as an *issue* been transformed since 1979 (irrespective of whether unemployment as a phenomenon has been transformed), but the nature of the 'unemployment game' (in the sense that the issue is played out by groups of competing actors) has itself been transformed. Whether by a well-developed plan or not, the government has in fact managed to introduce radical policy innovation, first of all with the active co-operation of the main interests and more recently without the co-operation of the Trades Union Congress (see below).

To a very large degree, the government has been preoccupied with its macro-economy strategy and with its desire to develop an increasingly competitive economy. There can be much argument about the effects of this strategy on unemployment itself, although Pissarides has pointed out that unemployment has 'exhibited a remarkable consistency in its behaviour for a very long time' (Pissarides, 1988, pp. 6–7). He argues that two particularly important facts need to be borne in mind when discussing unemployment.

1   Productivity growth and changes in aggregate demand do not

appear to affect unemployment on average over long periods of time.

2 For most of the time unemployment changes by small amounts, or even not at all. But there are some short periods of time when it changes fast.

(Pissarides, 1988, p. 7)

Of relevance to our earlier discussion of productivity growth is Pissarides's comment that 'a model which claims to have a plausible theory of unemployment must be consistent with the observations that over long periods of time, changes in labour productivity are reflected in changes in wages and not changes in unemployment' (Pissarides, 1988, p. 7). This view tends to lend support to our own contention that the government's strategies have not really been employment related. The policy goals such as industrial restructuring, increased competitiveness, greater flexibility in the labour market and increases in productivity are all necessary and laudable, but they may have no positive effect on unemployment in the short-term. Pissarides points out that the historical data confirm his view that unemployment generally changes by small amounts with occasional sudden shifts. Thus, 'unemployment fell quickly in the late 1930s and remained low until the late 1960s. It rose again quickly (but not by much) first in 1966 and then again in 1974 and remained at its high level until 1979. Another big rise took place in 1980–81, following which unemployment has remained more or less at that level since then' (Pissarides, 1988, p. 7). Central to his model is the argument that there are some things which can bring about quick and major changes in unemployment – called 'shocks' – and there is a mechanism which takes over after the initial shock and which stops unemployment from returning quickly to its prior level: what he calls 'unemployment persistence'.

Pissarides's analysis is especially interesting because it emphasizes supply-side factors as a greater cause of unemployment than demand factors: 'the higher unemployment that has persisted in Britain for seven or eight years . . . is due to supply-side reactions to the rise in unemployment itself. . . failures on the supply side cause much more output loss, through the under-utilization of resources, than the loss caused by aggregate demand failures' (Pissarides, 1988, p. 13). He explains the initial 'shock as being caused by a combination of unfavourable aggregate supply conditions abroad, OPEC II *and even worse aggregate demand conditions at home, brought about by the new*

Conservative Government' (Pissarides, 1988, p. 14, our emphasis). The key linkage between these conditions and unemployment is, he argues, the wage bargain. The nature of the wage bargain in Britain has allowed these shocks to be transmitted into unemployment and has allowed it to persist. The initial shock was certainly exacerbated by the Conservative government, which 'squeezed demand, which in the final analysis contributed more to the rise in unemployment than aggregate supply conditions did. *This is why 1980 was so much worse than 1974'* (Pissarides, 1988, p. 17, our emphasis). The supply-side responses that have caused the *persistence* of unemployment are threefold. First, he argues, the rise in long-term unemployment has actually contributed to the persistence of unemployment itself, because the long-term unemployed have become 'discouraged workers', withdrawing from active job search and with employers not keen to take them on – hence the fact that there are more vacancies now than in 1978, yet long-term unemployment is much greater. Secondly, he argues, *attitudes* (rather than the actual levels, which have been stable, in fact) towards social security have affected unemployed people's choosiness and the urgency with which they want to get back to work. Thirdly, he argues, unemployment has persisted via the nature of the wage bargain, because unemployed workers do not take part, the wage bargain being dominated by the wishes of senior employers and union officials. As evidence, he cites the fact that wages are rising fast even though we still have high unemployment.

The policy implications of Pissarides's thesis are interesting in the context of our study, concerned as it is with local responses to unemployment. In Chapter 5 we return to the question of the degree to which local actors can influence unemployment levels and to the importance of *central* action as a determinant of unemployment. But the Pissarides study does underline the role of central government in ameliorating or exacerbating economic trends. Thus his main policy prescription is one of *gradualism*, because 'gradual change in aggregate demand gives wage negotiators time to adjust before the next demand squeeze' (Pissarides, 1988, p. 20). The Conservative government did quite the wrong thing in 1980–1 in squeezing the economy sharply 'at a time when OPEC II called for a cushion to absorb the already negative supply shock' (Pissarides, 1988, p. 20). He concedes, however, that 'some governments may still want to do things quickly *for political reasons'* (Pissarides, 1988, p. 20) (our emphasis). This is similar to our own analysis that both national and local unemployment policies have to be understood in essentially political terms.

Pissarides's own prescriptions, too, have political implications – for example, that the unemployed should somehow be involved in the wage bargain, possibly via policies that encourage wage restraint (e.g. tax-based incomes policies), and subsidization of employment in order to reduce the cost of labour to the firm (Pissarides, 1988, p. 21). In a fascinating analysis, Pissarides is to some degree part of a widespread consenses – namely, that conscious *intervention* by government is necessary if unemployment is really to be cured rather than made 'acceptable' or 'massaged' away. It is to the broad style of the Conservative government's response, and to its most recent initiative, that we now turn.

Conservative 'management' of unemployment: a learning curve of radicalism?

One of the main difficulties in trying to develop a coherent characterization of the Conservative government's responses to unemployment is that the *range* of policies which potentially influence unemployment levels is enormous. For example, do we count monetary policy, taxation policy, exchange rate policy, interest rate policy, etc. as employment/unemployment policies, or should we just count specific anti-unemployment schemes such as YTS? (Even YTS might be seen as training policy rather than as unemployment policy). In practice, the variety of policies which more or less affect unemployment are generally linked by a philosophy which has become much clearer during the Conservative's period of office. This philosophy is summarized in the Department of Trade and Industry's White Paper, *The Department of Enterprise*, published in January 1988. This stated that 'The enterprise culture and the efficiency and competitiveness of industry and commerce need further encourage-ment. That is the role of the DTI.' The central themes were the promotion of open markets and individual enterprise. Yet this underlying philosophy, to which some major interests such as the trade unions have been bitterly opposed, has not prevented a whole succession of quite specific anti-unemployment measures, backed by large amounts of public expenditure. Moon has emphasized the degree of continuity and policy succession in anti-unemployment policies (Moon, 1983); and Moon and Richardson have traced the flow of policy changes, rapid by any standards, reflecting the growth of the problem facing governments: rising levels of unemployment, and the accompanying imperative upon successive governments to be seen to be doing something in response to the key political issue' (Moon & Richardson, 1985, p. 66). This almost bewildering succession of policy change is illustrated in Figure 1.1.

Since 1984 we have perhaps begun to see a break with policy succession and the emergence of a more determined attempt to shape events, rather than merely to react to them as part of a political holding operation. This shift is explicable in relation to two broader developments. First, the unemployment problem had been 'solved' by the 1987 general election, in that it was no longer a serious political threat for the government, even though it was then (and still is) at very high levels. Secondly, and more importantly, the government's attitude to the unemployment problem was similar to its attitudes to many other policy problems – namely, it had learned over time that it could actually *behave* as radically as it talked, and that radical policies could be forced through and on occasions might be popular. In this sense, the government has been on a 'learning curve of radicalism' – best demonstrated in the case of privatization, but also in such 'sacred' fields as the health service and regulation of the legal profession. The decline in the political importance of unemployment has coincided with a general increase in the confidence of the government that it could begin to attack long-established and hitherto 'franchised' policy areas and could risk the wrath of certain entrenched interests. An additional factor was that a long period of resource squeeze and austerity has made many of these interests much more susceptible either to downright bullying or usually to more sophisticated attempts at persuading them to consider radical policy change.

This rather broad analysis is illustrated perfectly by the introduction in 1983 of the Technical and Vocational Education Inititiative (TVEI). The origins of the new policy were quite different to the usual educational policy style as described by Kogan and others (Kogan, 1978). Consultation and negotiation were not the norm. Instead, the devisers of TVEI were anxious to act quickly in order to avoid having their ideas swallowed in a consultative morass (Moon and Richardson, 1984, p. 25). As the then Manpower Services Commission (MSC) Chairman, Lord Young (now Secretary of State for Trade and Industry), commented: 'Supposing we had decided to launch a debate about technical education, or the lack of it. We might have had a Royal Commission and it might have taken five years or even ten to get off the ground. Now we have a pilot project due to start by September next year' (*The Times*, 22 November 1982). TVEI could be

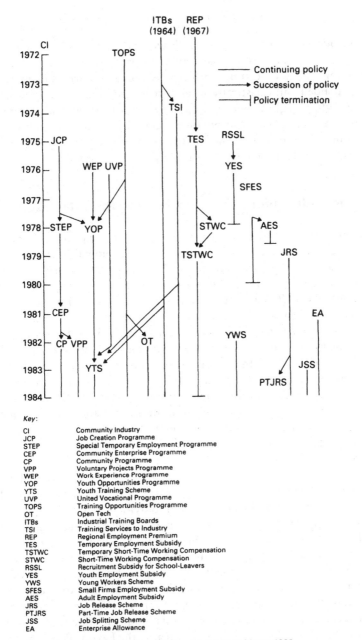

Key:

CI	Community Industry
JCP	Job Creation Programme
STEP	Special Temporary Employment Programme
CEP	Community Enterprise Programme
CP	Community Programme
VPP	Voluntary Projects Programme
WEP	Work Experience Programme
YOP	Youth Opportunities Programme
YTS	Youth Training Scheme
UVP	United Vocational Programme
TOPS	Training Opportunities Programme
OT	Open Tech
ITBs	Industrial Training Boards
TSI	Training Services to Industry
REP	Regional Employment Premium
TES	Temporary Employment Subsidy
TSTWC	Temporary Short-Time Working Compensation
STWC	Short-Time Working Compensation
RSSL	Recruitment Subsidy for School-Leavers
YES	Youth Employment Subsidy
YWS	Young Workers Scheme
SFES	Small Firms Employment Subsidy
AES	Adult Employment Subsidy
JRS	Job Release Scheme
PTJRS	Part-Time Job Release Scheme
JSS	Job Splitting Scheme
EA	Enterprise Allowance

Source: Moon and Richardson, 1985; adapted from Moon, 1983.

Figure 1.1   Policy change in job creation, work experience, training and employment subsidy schemes, 1972–84.

introduced in this way (albeit followed by a more traditional means of *implementation*, via consultation) in part because the education sector had gone through a long period of resource squeeze and responded enthusiastically to almost *any* scheme which looked as though it might deliver new resources. Also, many such interests have been gradually thrown on the defensive since 1979 and so are, in any case, much weakened in their resistance to policies which they might have opposed most vigorously in earlier periods.

The trades unions: from the inner to the outer circle?

This weakening of interests during a period of economic decline is no more evident than with the trades union movement. Indeed, it now appears that the trades unions – at least in the shape of the Trades Union Congress (TUC) – may have been in a logical trap since 1979. Thus, the TUC has consistently opposed the government's broad economic strategy. Equally consistently it has been at the same time an active *supporter* of the government's strategy by facilitating the 'management' of the unemployment problem by assisting in the implementation of the government's anti-unemployment policies. This it has done, until autumn 1988, by its co-operation (some would say collaboration) with the main anti-unemployment schemes such as the Youth Opportunities Programme (YOP), the Youth Training Scheme (and the extended YTS) and the Community Programme. It was felt by all (including the Government) that these schemes could not be delivered without TUC – and of course Confederation of British Industries (CBI) – co-operation, and this gave the TUC a degree of leverage at the implementation stage. This was especially so when the political salience of unemployment was very high. Even at the height of political salience, however, the TUC had little choice but to co-operate. In the first place, the TUC had as much genuine concern for the plight of the unemployed as anyone else had. Secondly, it could not afford to be seen to be refusing to assist in youth training programmes and in programmes intended to occupy and retrain the adult unemployed, when public concern was so high. Even if it could afford to stand the resultant obloquy itself, it could not risk the inevitable damage to its political ally, the Labour Party, because it felt that only the Labour Party would introduce an alternative economic strategy less likely to exacerbate the demand factors discussed above.

Employers, of course, faced an apparently less serious dilemma. In any case, they were engaged in much 'system-maintaining' behaviour (see Chapter 6) and, though they often disagreed with key elements of the government's economic strategy, they, like the TUC, could not contemplate the alternative being presented by other political parties. At a more practical level, employers were gaining measurable benefits from schemes such as YTS. For example, Deakin and Pratten (1987, p. 497) report that 'YTS reduces the costs to employers of training and employing young people' and that 'the scheme does not distort competition between firms.' Some 42 per cent of sampled firms that were participating in YTS replied that 'the schemes had helped them to improve the training that they provided'. In particular, certain industries (e.g. retailing and hotels) benefited because 'some firms did not have formal training schemes before the introduction of YTS' (Deakin and Pratten, 1987, p. 496). Similarly, Manpower Services Commission (MSC) figures indicate positive rates of return for firms' participation in YTS. The MSC is reported as claiming that 'In about 85% of traineeships, in which companies provide foundation training, employers benefit by an average of almost £400 per trainee over the YTS year' (*Financial Times*, 8 February 1988). Clearly, the employers are obtaining selective benefits in participating in schemes like YTS, as well as contributing to a public good.

The irony is that most of the other interests attracted into participation in the 'unemployment industry' were actually not the government's allies at all, but were its political opponents. Yet their very participation enabled the anti-unemployment schemes 'to work' in the sense that the schemes seemingly reassured the electorate that 'something was being done' and at the same time reduced the size of that symbolic but crucial figure – the total number of unemployed in any month. Michael Meacher's (1988) attack on the 'fiddles behind the jobless totals', discussed earlier, neglects to point out that many of these 'fiddles' could not have been perpetrated without the active (if not willing) co-operation of the TUC itself. For example, he cites the example of 350,000 YTS trainees being counted as employed, but does not point out that YTS could never have got off the ground if the TUC had not been in active co-operation, via its membership of the MSC – in terms of both the inception of the scheme and its eventual implementation. Moreover, the TUC has continually pressed (and with some degree of success) for *improvements* in the scheme – in particular for a major increase in the amount and quality of *training* provided. In so far as YTS has improved and has become more acceptable, that is is part due to the TUC's own efforts.

The difficulty for the TUC and other interests not well disposed towards the government's strategy for unemployment (a strategy which was not *really* related to unemployment but part of its pursuit of other goals, as we have argued) is that they always had to make a fine judgement as to how far to take opposition to the details of any particular scheme. Events during 1988 illustrate this 'decision trap' clearly. One year earlier, in June 1987, the TUC had decided to withdraw from the Job Training Scheme (a new work-experience and training programme for young unemployed people). Although not a major scheme (designed to provide 10,000 places for jobless young people aged between 18 and 25), it provoked TUC opposition and ultimate withdrawal, because the TUC objected to the rates being paid to the trainees, to the amount of training being provided and because of a general lack of resources for the programme. No major consequences befell the TUC on that occasion, but the post-election developments relating to the new Employment Training (ET) scheme proved to be of much greater importance.

ET, estimated to cost £1.5 billion per year, is designed to unify over thirty existing schemes for the adult unemployed. The two major schemes – the Community Programme and the ill-fated Job Training Scheme – are now integrated into ET, and in total ET is to provide for 600,000 people per year. Such a large scheme demands union co-operation, since so many places cannot be found unless large manufacturing companies and local authorities are involved, both sectors being heavily unionized. In the run-up to the launch of the scheme, the key issues were the level of payments to trainees, the plan to improve training without an overall increase in resources, the curtailed role of unions in vetting schemes and the limited employment rights of trainees. In the event, the TUC withdrew from the scheme in September 1988, despite pleas from the Labour leader Mr Kinnock. The decision itself caused divisions within the TUC and has led the government to transfer the main functions of the Training Commission (formerly the MSC) to a new agency within the Employment Department Group and to propose the abolition of the Training Commission itself. (The removal of the Commission's main functions was necessary because the Secretary of State, Mr Fowler, did not have statutory authority to remove the TUC, since any change in the status and composition of the Commission requires primary legislation. Hence, removal of the function was the only means of sanctioning the TUC). Not only were the Commission's main functions removed to the executive agency within the Employment Department Group, but the Area Manpower Boards, on which the TUC is represented, are also due to be disbanded. This does not necessarily mean that union involvement in anti-unemployment schemes is at an end. In his statement Mr Fowler indicated that he wanted 'to secure the *effective* involvement of employers and other organizations – such as voluntary organizations, local authorities and their schools and colleges, and individual trade unions – which wish to play a *constructive* role in the delivery of these programmes' (*Employment Gazette*, October 1988, p. 544, our emphasis).

The exclusion of the TUC in fact brings to an end a long period of union integration into the work of the MSC since its formation in 1974. With the exception of the 1987 withdrawal from JTS, the TUC had usually managed to negotiate concessions, via the tripartite tradition of the MSC/Training Commission, which it considered sufficient for it to remain on board. Indeed, in the case of ET, the individual union members of the Commission had initially approved the scheme, and had gained significant concessions from the government, only to find the TUC Council rejecting the scheme. In that sense, the TUC dug a hole for itself in pressing its objections to the scheme when it was known that the government would remove the TUC's participation from the Commission altogether if the TUC refused to co-operate with ET. Whether or not one accepts that the TUC dug its own grave or whether one believes that the government set a trap into which the TUC fell, the TUC has now lost its 'remaining toe-hold on political influence by seeing the MSC [*sic*] reconstituted and drawn back into the Department of Employment' (*Financial Times*, 25 May 1988). Having shifted from having a virtual veto over the development of schemes in the earlier years of the MSC (and even in the earlier years of the Conservative government), the TUC first saw its representation on the MSC reduced and then, by its own actions (admittedly under duress), became an outsider group. It had moved from the inner to the outer circles in just a few years, *even though unemployment has remained very high and has clearly not been 'solved' in any real sense.*

Having found itself almost totally without influence, the TUC is now showing signs of trying to limit the damage to itself. Thus, in mid-October 1988 it was reported that the TUC would advise unions to 'use discretion' on ET, based on a report from the TUC's Education and Training Committee and its Employment and Organization

Committee, suggesting that individual unions should decide whether to participate in the scheme. Of particular concern was the threat to the employment of full-time workers who ran the various anti-unemployment schemes, if the schemes fell significantly short of the recruiting targets which the government had set. Rather like the hundreds of voluntary bodies which had expanded their organizations and staffing in order to participate in the delivery of YTS and the Community Programme, the unions themselves also had thousands of members employed in delivering training and organizing schemes and had, therefore, developed some kind of dependency relationship. Having voted against co-operating with ET in September 1988, the TUC by the end of October 1988 had begun to recognize the costs of non-participation and began to advise its officials that they could co-operate with ET under certain conditions. For example, the construction industry union UCCATT, the TGWU, the GMB and the AEU were all engaged in detailed discussions with bodies such as the Training Agency, the Engineering Industry Training Board and the Construction Industry Training Board regarding participation in ET.

Breaking the dependency relationship has had relatively severe consequences for the TUC, turning it into a peripheral actor. The choice between active integration – which itself assisted the government's policital objectives – and exit, which gives the unions no influence whatsoever, is a difficult one to make. The choice which has been made not only excludes the TUC from influencing what happens to ET but, more importantly perhaps, opens up a greater possibility for the government to introduce a much more radical approach to unemployment and training.

A new era in unemployment policy?

Even prior to the TUC's withdrawal from ET and its rapid exclusion from all other schemes, there were signs that the government was moving towards a major shift in emphasis in its specific anti-unemployment programmes. Although officially rejecting US-style 'workfare' schemes, much of the more recent policy development has been rather less like the policy succession described by Moon (1983) and more akin to workfare-type programmes, albeit still with some significant differences. The trend has been to increase the pressure on the unemployed either to find work or to join training schemes – for example, by withdrawing benefit from unemployed young people if they refuse to join YTS and by withdrawing benefit from those who refuse a Restart job interview.

While workfare still seems a long way off in Britain (despite a rather favourable study sponsored by the Department of Employment itself), developments in Scotland in the autumn of 1988 appeared to presage a major shift in the mechanism by which the range of interventions, designed ultimately to reduce unemployment, are delivered. The crux of the new policy is that the work of the Scottish Development Agency and the Training Commission should be combined into one body, possibly called Scottish Enterprise. It would concentrate on industrial training and would work through local agencies in which business people would play the leading role (Scottish Office, 1988). Conceived by the Chairman of CBI Scotland, Bill Hughes, the plan received the tentative backing of the Scottish TUC and even of the Labour Party in Scotland, despite some misgivings within the Scottish CBI itself.

The fact that the very radical Hughes plan was adopted in principle so quickly (he first launched the idea in June 1988, and the Prime Minister accepted it in her speech to the CBI in Glasgow in September 1988) is an illustration of our thesis that there has been an accelerating shift in the style of policy-making in the anti-unemployment field. Thus, one of the main interests has now been excluded from the national-level institutional arrangements, and quite radical organizational and policy-content changes appear to be under way. It is also illustrative of a longer-term trend towards emphasizing *local* initiatives and *local* delivery. Perhaps the most interesting feature of the Hughes plan is its concentration on the decentralized delivery of assistance and training via local agencies. As Mrs Thatcher put it, the core of the Hughes plan was the linking of enterprise and training 'not only at the top through a single organization but, even more important, at the local level' (*Financial Times*, 10 September 1988). In practical terms, the Secretary of State for Scotland, Mr Rifkind, envisages 'local agencies with full-time professional staff reporting to a committee consisting of businessmen, with possibly also trade unionists and local authority representatives who would draw up schemes and send them to Scottish Enterprise for approval' (*Financial Times*, 10 September 1988). Similarly, a leading participant in Scottish Business in the Community (ScotBIC) has commented that 'Almost certainly the mechanism chosen to deliver the overall policy of engendering an enterprise culture will embrace the one-door approach, be private-sector led, and be local-community aimed and driven' (Stevenson, 1988, p. 4). The status and power of actors, the decison-making processes and the policies themselves have begun to look very different to the decade or more of MSC tripartism. The death knell of tripartism has signalled the shift towards a greater centralization – in the sense of a firmer ministerial grip on policy – combined with a decentralization of powers to local bodies (but not to local *authorities*). It is local bodies that are likely to be responsible for delivery of training and anti-unemployment programmes, opening up opportunities for a further redrawing of the power structure in this policy area. Thus, at least one interest, the Association of British Chambers of Commerce, was quick to seize the opportunity presented by the demise of the Training Commission and the exit of the TUC to argue for devolution of powers to local bodies and for a national advisory body 'more representative of employers and employees than the Training Commission' (*Financial Times*, 26 September 1988).

In Scotland at least, this major shift in national policies has provoked a considerable debate within those organizations which are the subject-matter of this book – namely, enterprise trusts or agencies. It has done so because the initiative has highlighted two central core themes in the development of the government's anti-unemployment policies: the emphasis on a *business/entrepreneurial culture* and increasing emphasis on *devolving responsibility to the local level*. The more recent policy developments which we have described are in fact linked with *economic* developments. Economic conditions have created the necessary *political* environment for these more radical policies to be given a much greater thrust. Without the positive (albeit with many qualifications) economic developments such as increased economic growth, rising productivity and an economic upturn, the government would have been unable to have effected the exit of the TUC from all influence at the national level and would have been unable to contemplate a much more determined shift of responsibility to the private sector and to local communities. Moreover, it would have been unable to contemplate the development of further mechanisms of local delivery if there had not already been a decade of experience of local partnership schemes. Such schemes are the subject-matter of the rest of this book.

References

Brookings Institution (1980), *Britain's Economic Performance* (Washington, DC: Brookings Institution).

Confederation of British Industry (1988), *Quarterly Survey* (London: CBI).

Deakin, B. M., and Pratten, C. F. (1987), 'Economic effects of YTS', *Employment Gazette*, October, pp. 491–7.

Department of Trade and Industry (1988), *The Department for Enterprise*, Cmnd 278 (London: HMSO).

Fenstein, Charles (1989), 'Benefits of backwardness and costs of continuity', in A. Seldon and A. Graham (eds), *Comparative Postwar Economic Performance* (London: Routledge).

Gomulka, S. (1979), 'Britain's slow industrial growth–increasing inefficiency versus low rate of technical change', in W. Beckerman (ed.), *Slow Growth in Britain, Consensus and Consequences.* (Oxford: Clarendon Press), pp. 166–93.

Jowell, R. (ed.), *British Social Attitudes: Fifth Report* (1988), Social and Community Planning Research (Aldershot: Gower).

Kogan, M. (1978), *Politics of Educational Change* (Glasgow: Fontana).

Meacher, M. (1988), 'UK unemployment. The fiddles behind the jobless totals', *Financial Times*, 14 September.

Meen, G. (1988), 'International comparisons of the UK's long-run economic performance,' *Oxford Review of Economic Policy*, spring, pp. xxii, xli.

Moon, J. (1983), 'Policy change in direct government response to UK unemployment', *Journal of Public Policy*, vol. 3, no. 3, pp. 301–29.

Moon, J., and Richardson, J. J. (1984a), 'The unemployment industry', *Policy and Politics*, vol. 12, no. 2, pp. 391–411.

Moon, J. and Richardson, J. J. (1984b), 'Policy making with a difference? The Technical and Vocational Education Initiative', *Public Administration*, vol. 62, spring, pp. 23–33).

Moon, J. and Richardson, J. J. (1985), *Unemployment in the UK: Politics and Policies* (Aldershot: Gower).

OECD (1987), *Historical Statistics 1960–85* (Paris: OECD).

OECD (1988) *Employment Report* (Paris: OECD).

PA Consulting Group (1988), *UK Productivity – Closing the Gap* (London: PA Consulting Group).

Pissarides, C. A. (1988), *Unemployment and Macroeconomics. An Inaugural Lecture*, Discussion Paper No. 34 (London: Centre for Labour Economics, London School of Economics).

Richardson, J. J., and Moon, J. (1984), 'The politics of unemployment in the UK', *Political Quarterly*, vol. 55, no. 1, Jan–March, pp. 29–37.

Scottish Office (1988), *Scottish Enterprise: A New Approach to Training and Enterprise Creation*, Cm 534 (Edinburgh: HMSO).

Stevenson, B. (1988), Introduction to debate on the 'Hughes initiative', Scottish Business in the Community Dunblane Conference, October.

Wolf, M. (1988), 'Is there a British miracle?', *Financial Times*, 16 September.

2 Local dimensions of a national problem

Introduction

Two features stand out in any cursory examination of local economic problems in the UK: first, the differential distribution of the problems of decline and unemployment. The spatial patterns of the problem are markedly uneven. There has been considerable popular debate about the North-versus-South divide based on social and economic divergences and political differences. How accurate is this picture? What other factors are at work influencing the distribution of unemployment?

The second marked trend is the explosion of local economic strategies and forms of intervention. Not all local strategies are the responsibility of local authorities. There is a growing conflict between central and local government in the UK, reversing the consensus between the levels of government in the UK, reversing the consensus between the levels of government which Bulpitt (1983) shows has characterized the UK during most of the twentieth century. National governments have become more concerned with the impact of local authorities on the national economy and have sought to control expenditure (Stoker, 1988). At the same time there has been a growing dissatisfaction on the part of the centre with the political direction of the metropolitan urban authorities and what is seen as their resistance to central government policies. The conflict has taken two forms: first, a political struggle by certain local authorities resisting central government policies such as rate capping. The most intensive conflict was that between Liverpool and Whitehall (Parkinson, 1986). The second form of resistance has been the development of alternative models of policy, and nowhere is this more noticeable than in the development of local economic strategies which offer an alternative model to the dominant central government market-based model (Boddy and Fudge, 1984).

This chapter falls into two main parts. In the first we examine the evidence for spatial disparities in economic growth and the problem of unemployment in order to highlight the scale of polarization. In the second part we examine the political response to the problem of the local economy and in particular alternative strategies at the local level.

The spatial economy: regional disparities

The issue of spatial disparities in economic performance and the uneven distribution of unemployment is not a new one. In the UK regional policy came on to the policy agenda in the 1930s as the older industrial areas which had been at the heart of the Industrial Revolution began to experience decline (Maclennan and Parr, 1979). The gravitation of economic activity to the South-East and the Midlands was a marked trend in the post-1945 period despite the development of regional incentives to encourage a reverse flow.

The trends, however, were not simply regional but also involved a shift from the metropolitan urban core to the outer conurbations and smaller towns. Such change has been well documented. For example, Drewett, Goddard and Spence (1976) chart the loss of population and employment from the urban core since the 1960s.

There was thus a regional and urban shift. Not surprisingly the urban centres in the declining regions suffered even more. Analysis by Wolman (1987) shows a statistical link between the performance of the regional economy and the performance of urban economies within the region. This is confirmed by Begg and Moore (1987). Analysing changes in employment in the 100 largest cities in the UK they compiled tables of the 20 fastest-growing and the 20 slowest-growing cities. Not surprisingly the good performers were located largely in the South-East, although there were exceptions; for example, because of the oil industry Aberdeen was one of the fastest-growing cities. The 20 poorest performers were located mainly in the North-East and North-West of England, Scotland and Wales, but also included the Midlands and Thames Estuary.

Thus, while no simple picture emerges there are broad regional patterns which do give some substance to the argument that there is a North–South divide, although we must include an increasing part of the UK as 'North'. For example, one of the most remarkable declines in economic performance and growth in unemployment has been in the West Midlands. Spencer *et al.* (1986) show that for the period 1945–66 unemployment rarely rose above 1 per cent. In 1985 it was 17 per cent. Similarly, Young and Mills (1983) document the loss of jobs in Greater London in the context of regional growth in the South-East during the period 1961–78. Over this period London lost 17 per cent of its employment, with particularly heavy losses in the manufacturing sector amounting to nearly half of the employment in that sector. At the same time England and Wales lost 4 per cent of employment. In contrast, the South-East region increased its manufacturing employment by 10 per cent and overall employment by 12 per cent.

The complex distributional pattern of unemployment was examined by Armstrong and Riley (1987) in an article which challenged the simplistic nature of the debate on the North–South divide. They argued that if one looked simply at overall rates of unemployment then a North–South division could be sustained. However, if one took a wider view of economic performance, including long-term unemployment, female activity rates, GDP, earnings and benefits, then a more complex pattern emerged. They argued that there was a patchwork effect, with areas of low unemployment in the North – for example, North Yorkshire and Grampian (Aberdeen) – while there were pockets of high unemployment in the South – for example, the Isle of Wight and Kent. However, they argued that broad regional analysis could be misleading, and one needed to take account of the distribution of population in urban areas. This showed that only 2 per cent of workers in the Northern regional travel-to-work area worked in areas where unemployment was under 10 per cent, whereas the corresponding figure for the South-East was 39 per cent. Only 0.5 per cent of the South-East workforce were in travel-to-work areas with unemployment rates of over 20 per cent, in contrast to 35 per cent in the North.

In comparing metropolitan areas, Armstrong and Riley show that despite the problems of the London conurbation it still had lower unemployment than Northern metropolitan areas. They concluded that even a more complex multivariate analysis, rather than simple unemployment rates, showed that the North faced severe economic problems and that controversy about the North–South divide was often 'trivial and pedantic':

> The fact that the 'North' is a misnomer (since it includes Wales and should also probably include parts of the South-West) is not important. The lack of a static linear boundary between North and

South should not distract us from the key issues. Regional disparities are far worse than at any other time in the post-war period.

(Armstrong and Riley, 1987, pp. 100–1)

The North has lost more manufacturing jobs and not gained sufficient service-sector jobs to compensate. A more detailed account of how this has affected one region is provided by the 'State of the Region' reports produced annually by the North of England County Councils Association (NECCA). In 1985 NECCA produced a review report looking back to the first report of 1977 to record economic and social trends in the region over this period. The region had lost one-third of its manufacturing workforce, or 146,000 jobs, between 1977 and 1985. In total 230,000 jobs were lost, representing a decline of 20 per cent. Other indicators such as GDP, investment and small firm formation all showed lower levels of performance than the national average. The North was one of three regions where growth in the services sector failed to offset decline in manufacturing, and it was the only region where employment in services was lower in 1984 than it had been in 1977, by 9,000 (NECCA, 1986).

Official figures confirm these disparities. In 1987 the Department of Employment published the results of its 1984 Census of Employment. This showed that over the period 1981–4 only the South-West and East Anglia had gained jobs, while other regions varied markedly

Table 2.1 Employees in employment in Great Britain, 1981, 1984 and 1986 (thousands)

Region	Sept. 1981	Census 1984	Change 1981–4	June 1986	Index: Sept. 1984 = 100
South-East	7,245	7,219	−26	7,342	101.7
East Anglia	681	717	+36	762	106.2
South-West	1,546	1,553	+7	1,569	101.1
West Midlands	2,033	1,981	−52	2,020	102.0
East Midlands	1,467	1,457	−10	1,517	104.1
Yorkshire and Humberside	1,843	1,774	−69	1,777	100.2
North-West	2,454	2,296	−158	2,261	98.5
North	1,119	1,060	−59	1,077	101.6
Wales	937	886	−51	858	96.8
Scotland	1,985[a]	1,905	−80	1,887	99.1
Great Britain	21,309[a]	20,846	−563	21,070	101.1

[a] Revised.

Source: derived from Department of Employment, 1987, table 3, p. 33, and table 1.5, p. S13.

in their decline from a loss of 10,000 jobs in the East Midlands to a loss of 158,000 in the North-West. Updating the figures by comparing 1984 with 1986 did show a general improvement in that only three regions (the North-West, Wales and Scotland) continued to lose jobs, but conversely only East Anglia and the Midlands showed any significant improvement in their performance. Most regions made marginal improvements (Table 2.1).

Turning to unemployment, we can see a similar pattern, with areas such as East Anglia and the South-East recording consistently under the national average throughout the 1980s, while the North shows well above average rates (Table 2.2). Another indicator of relative decline is the level of notified redundancies.

Table 2.3 shows the trend in redundancies over the period 1979–87 by region. The impact of the 1980–1 recession is highlighted by the

Table 2.2   Unemployment by region (including school-leavers), 1982–8 (thousands)

Region	1982	1983	1984	1985	1986	1987	1988 (July)
South-East	664.6	721.4	748.0	782.4	784.7	680.5	494.8
	(7.7%)	(8.4%)	(8.4%)	(8.6%)	(8.6%)	(7.3%)	(5.3%)
East Anglia	72.2	77.5	77.3	81.3	83.4	72.5	49.3
	(8.5%)	(9.0%)	(8.7%)	(8.8%)	(8.6%)	(7.1%)	(4.9%)
South-West	179.0	188.6	193.7	204.9	205.7	178.9	129.0
	(9.1%)	(9.7%)	(9.7%)	(10.2%)	(10.0%)	(10.0%)	(6.3%)
West Midlands	337.9	354.7	345.4	349.7	346.7	305.9	235.9
	(13.6%)	(14.5%)	(14.1%)	(14.1%)	(13.3%)	(11.6%)	(9.0%)
East Midlands	176.6	188.0	194.3	202.3	202.8	183.9	145.7
	(9.9%)	(10.7%)	(10.9%)	(11.3%)	(10.6%)	(9.4%)	(7.3%)
Yorkshire and Humberside	273.2	288.7	291.9	305.8	315.9	286.0	231.7
	(12.2%)	(13.0%)	(12.9%)	(13.3%)	(13.4%)	(12.0%)	(9.6%)
North-West	407.8	437.1	442.9	452.0	448.3	403.3	328.8
	(13.6%)	(14.6%)	(14.5%)	(14.6%)	(14.8%)	(13.4%)	(10.9%)
North	214.6	225.7	230.5	237.6	234.9	213.1	176.7
	(15.5%)	(16.7%)	(17.0%)	(17.3%)	(16.1%)	(14.7%)	(12.2%)
Wales	164.8	170.4	173.3	180.6	179.0	157.0	126.1
	(13.8%)	(14.2%)	(14.2%)	(14.6%)	(14.7%)	(13.1%)	(10.6%)
Scotland	318.0	335.6	341.6	353.0	359.8	345.8	290.5
	(13.0%)	(13.7%)	(13.8%)	(14.0%)	(14.4%)	(13.9%)	(11.7%)
Great Britain[1]	2,808.5	2,987.6	3,038.4	3,149.4	3,161.3	2,826.9	2,208.5
	(10.8%)	(11.5%)	(11.5%)	(11.7%)	(11.6%)	(10.3%)	(8.0%)

Note:
[1] Great Britain summary is derived from a different source to the regional breakdown so figures do not strictly add up.

Source: Department of Employment, 1987, table 2.3, pp. S20–2, and table 2.1, p. S18; and 1988, table 2.3, p. S20–2, and table 2.1, p. S1A.

Table 2.3 Confirmed redundancies by region, 1979–87

Region	1979	1980	1981	1982	1983	1984	1985	1986	1987
South-East	26,798	70,015	105,878	80,300	58,345	42,074	34,853	39,284	19,850
East Anglia	2,981	7,554	11,463	6,471	4,165	2,356	3,544	5,001	2,168
South West	11,031	26,598	30,998	24,898	23,777	14,758	12,829	16,509	13,553
West Midlands	19,320	69,436	59,556	40,229	40,413	25,675	27,653	22,645	12,648
East Midlands	8,449	40,959	33,720	29,449	23,259	20,643	17,228	21,283	14,974
Yorkshire and Humberside	17,838	50,879	63,102	45,957	37,807	26,570	32,400	27,151	15,866
North-West	40,705	92,596	91,739	67,117	51,091	37,935	35,784	40,132	23,244
North	14,985	33,276	40,103	32,424	30,274	25,727	23,579	22,679	13,910
Wales	11,663	45,215	36,432	24,647	16,041	11,441	14,602	11,359	5,089
Scotland	33,014	57,178	59,039	48,944	41,538	30,164	24,856	31,958	22,833
Great Britain	186,784	493,704	532,070	400,416	326,638	237,343	227,328	238,001	144,135

Source: Department of Employment, 1987; table 2.30, p. S38; 1988, table 2.30, p. S41.

enormous leaps in redundancies through the country, but at the same time some regions clearly suffered more from rationalization and business failures than others. Interestingly, several regions were losing more jobs annually in 1985 through redundancies than they had been in 1979, although at a far lower level than the peak years of 1980–1. The idea that the South-East is isolated from these trends is also shown to be false. The bulk of job loss in the region is accounted for by Greater London. The decline of previously buoyant areas is illustrated in these figures. For example, the West Midlands was still suffering higher annual redundancies in 1986 than in 1979. The table shows a major decline in declared redundancies in 1987, although regional disparities remain; for example, the North-West and Scotland continued to suffer marked job losses.

Finally, Table 2.4 shows the performance in terms of employees in employment by region in different sectors of the economy. The data reveal the continued decline of the manufacturing sector since the Census of Employment except in East Anglia. The service sector has shown growth in all regions since 1984, but again the rate of growth varies from regions significantly above the national rate such as East Anglia and the Midlands to regions with only marginal growth such as Wales and the North-West.

Analysis by the Department of Trade and Industry based on a report to the EEC gave assumptions about employment and industry to the 1990s. It revealed that the government did not expect regional disparities to reduce significantly (Naughtie, 1986). While the document was described as a series of 'working assumptions' rather than a forecast, it provided a clue to government thinking about likely trends in the UK spatial economy. The report made depressing reading, offering little prospect for sustained growth and reduced unemployment in the regions.

This scenario was confirmed in a report by Cambridge Econometrics and the Northern Ireland Research Centre. It predicted that the North, the North-West and Northern Ireland would continue to suffer job loss and population decline until the end of the century (Cambridge Econometrics, 1987). The report examined what might happen to the regions if the national economy grew at an annual average rate of 4 per cent. It predicted that even in these circumstances unemployment would remain high in the peripheral regions. For example, in Northern Ireland it predicted that 12.4% per cent would be unemployed as against the UK's rate of 2.7 per cent and East Anglia's 0.6 per cent.

Table. 2.4 Employees in employment by region and sector; June 1986 (thousands)

Region	Total all sectors	Index: Sept. '84 = 100	Production and construction	Index: Sept. '84 = 100	Production	Index: Sept. '84 = 100	Manufacturing	Index: Sept. '84 = 100	Services	Index: Sept '84 = 100
South-East	7,342	101.7	1,786	93.6	1,499	93.9	1,395	93.9	5,488	104.8
East Anglia	762	106.2	247	104.6	210	105.3	201	106.0	481	108.9
South-West	1,569	101.1	464	98.0	400	99.2	374	99.5	1,062	103.0
West Midlands	2,020	102.0	834	98.5	746	98.6	703	99.2	1,158	104.9
East Midlands	1,517	104.1	632	100.1	572	100.4	497	101.8	854	107.8
Yorkshire and Humberside	1,777	100.2	628	92.7	541	92.5	460	94.9	1,122	105.2
North-West	2,261	98.5	792	94.3	682	94.2	634	94.5	1,454	101.1
North	1,077	101.6	380	96.2	324	96.8	270	97.9	684	105.1
Wales	858	96.8	283	91.2	240	91.3	202	95.0	554	100.1
Scotland	1,887	99.1	598	93.8	464	93.1	412	94.9	1,258	102.3
Great Britain	21,070	101.1	6,145	95.5	5,678	95.7	5,148	96.6	14,116	104.2

Source: Department of Employment, 1987, table 1.5, p. S13.

The spatial economy: the urban dimension

Having looked at the evidence for regional disparities in a little detail, we now turn to the urban dimension. The 'inner city' is a phrase which has assumed enormous political significance as a problem for all governments since the 1970s. Hasluck (1987) draws on a wealth of data to show how metropolitan areas have lost population and jobs since the 1960s, with particularly sharp decline during the late 1970s. For example, between 1971 and 1981 Great Britain lost 2.7 per cent of its jobs, against Greater London's loss of 24.5% per cent, Merseyside's 13.5 per cent and the West Midlands' 10.8 per cent. Within the metropolitan area the inner city has suffered the worst decline. Hausner and Robson (1986) show the relative loss of jobs between the inner cities and outer areas. Between 1971 and 1981 inner cities declined by 14.6 per cent against a decline of 7.1 per cent for outer cities and 5.4 per cent for free-standing towns. Small towns and rural areas showed an increase of 3.5 per cent.

Even when local urban labour markets are 'job rich' – that is, having a greater number of jobs than the local labour force – local unemployment could remain high because of mismatches between the unemployed and jobs in terms of skills, training and the influx of non-residents. McArthur (1987) has highlighted this problem in relation to Clydeside, where special initiatives in stimulating the local economy of small areas within the conurbation did not have a substantial impact on levels of unemployment in these areas because most of the jobs went to non-residents.

The performance of the urban area is also affected by changes in the structure of the economy and demand for labour. The general shift away from manufacturing towards services has had profound effects on spatial patterns of economic activity and on the composition of the workforce (Hasluck, 1987). Put crudely, urban core areas historically dependent on manufacturing industries have suffered more than outer areas or other locations which have good service-sector employment. The growth of service-sector employment in the inner city has not been enough to compensate. The changes in the urban economy have been enormous. In a twenty-year period from 1961 to 1981 Glasgow has moved from having an industrial economy with 60 per cent of its labour force in manufacturing to a service economy with 60 per cent of its labour force in service industries (Lever and Mather, 1986). This pattern is reflected in other conurbations.

Locational factors have also been cited to explain urban decline. In particular, the costs associated with expansion for businesses in inner areas and the physical constraints on buildings and land have been seen as significant in leading to relocation by firms (Fothergill and Gudgin, 1982; Young and Mills, 1983). Other factors include the lack of a dynamic small firms base, reflecting in part historical dependencies on a few big employers in traditional industries which failed to provide a seedbed for entrepreneurs (Checkland, 1976). Another important factor is the concentration of the more disadvantaged within the urban core. Unemployment is influenced by age, ethnic origin and educational attainment. Urban areas have a marked concentration of long-term unemployment (Green, 1985).

Hasluck from his extensive analysis concluded starkly: 'Mass unemployment in Britain is largely an urban problem' (Hasluck, 1987, p. 96).

Policy responses

Responses by policy-makers to these problems will be influenced by their understanding of the causes and their capacity to make sense of their environment, what Young and Mills (1983) termed their 'assumptive worlds'. Several explanations have been put forward for economic decline and how this influences policy responses. For example, a major gap in the urban economy is seen as the lack of enterprise, particularly the low rates of small firm formation. This is based on an assumption that small firms are the major source of new jobs in the economy. Policy thus focuses on what can be done to stimulate new firms in the inner cities. Enterprise trusts are viewed as an important policy instrument in this scenario.

Another explanation is that excessive 'planning' and 'bureaucracy' have stifled growth and led firms to relocate. The prescription is to relax or abolish these 'contraints'. Enterprise Zones are one example of how this prescription has developed into a policy proposal. It also highlights the paradox of policy. Presented as an experiment in free market ideology, it is in fact a heavy financial subsidy to businesses within the zone, principally through the abolition of local rates for ten years.

Related to this explanation of 'bureaucracy' is the argument that local government is too slow in reaching decisions, lacks the organizational capacity to carry out major economic development programmes and is sometimes politically opposed to working with the private sector. One answer to this 'problem' has been to install Urban Development Corporations (UDCs) in certain areas to take over the planning and development functions of the local authorities.

From the opposite ideological perspective, several local authorities have argued that it is the lack of control and planning in the local economy that has caused the problems. Capital has disinvested because it no longer finds the inner city a profitable area to operate, leaving behind devastated communities which have no control over corporate decision-making. The answer is to create instruments which seek to subject capital to more control and public accountability through enterprise boards and to seek alternative collective forms of enterprise such as community businesses and worker co-operatives.

Policy models

How can we make sense of these conflicting views? Hasluck (1987) argues that there are three main types of policy response based on alternative theoretical perspectives concerning the causes of unemployment and economic change. The first he labels *neo-classical* or *competitive*. It is essentially a liberal market model where unemployment is seen as voluntary, frictional and seasonal, and caused by individual decisions of workers and firms. The set of policies advocated by this model is designed to improve the efficient operation of the market by encouraging incentives and removing 'artificial' barriers. The role of public intervention is to be kept to a minimum, largely providing the framework for the market to function. Paradoxically, this may lead to significant intervention – for example, trades union legislation or subsidies to capital through programmes such as Enterprise Zones.

The second approach is what Hasluck defines as a *structuralist/ Keynesian* approach. This is essentially a modification of the market. It acknowledges that some unemployment is not voluntary or frictional but structural and related to lack of demand in the economy. The market does fail, and therefore the state must intervene to rectify these weaknesses through active labour market policies (such as MSC training) and stimulating demand in the economy.

Finally, there is a *radical/Marxist* model which sees unemployment as a reflection of class conflict in the economy and the development of capitalism following the logic of accumulation, which increasingly requires restructuring to remain competitive. The policy response of this model is based on a major extension of public control over capital and seeking to change the relationship between capital and labour to the benefit of the latter.

The policy models and local economy

Responses to local problems may be seen as fundamentally dependent on centrally determined policy. The market perspective, for example, might emphasize the role of government in eliminating blockages in the market, such as trades union power or wage controls. Keynesian or structuralist approaches would see a role for national training schemes and for macro-economic demand management. The radical Marxist model clearly sees a systematic change as fundamental, based on state power over key economic decision-making.

At the same time, policy is increasingly localized. Problems are seen in spatial terms – the inner cities, the urban problem, regional imbalances – as well as in terms of markets or macro-economic policies (whether interventionist or non-interventionist). All political parties have placed increasing emphasis on local needs and local responses either as an alternative to central strategies or complementary to them. The market approach, which can be said broadly to guide the liberal economic policies of the Conservative governments under Margaret Thatcher, has increasingly stressed the importance of local public–private partnerships in stimulating an 'enterprise culture' in the inner cities. This raises problems for local authorities in how to respond since it represents in some cases a challenge to local control. Many of the problems in the local economy are seen as stemming from inefficient local governments: rate burdens on businesses, planning controls preventing private developments, ideological opposition to working with the private sector. At its most extreme the response from the centre is to displace local authorities by centrally appointed UDCs. The alternative consensus approach is to encourage local authorities to work closely with the private sector on specific projects, for example through Urban Devleopment Grants, or on providing support for new enterprise development through enterprise trusts.

The structuralist/Keynesian approach, which might broadly describe the policy stance of the Labour opposition, sees local authorities as vital actors in developing economic policies which can complement national strategies. Before the 1987 general election there was considerable debate within the Labour party about the contribution of local authorities to economic regeneration through direct intervention in the local economy (enterprise boards investing in firms) and through expanding services (direct job creation with multiplier impacts on local demand) (Bennington, 1986).

The enterprise boards were a major development in local authority intervention in the economy. They were developed by certain 'radical' Labour-controlled urban authorities in the early 1980s. Most local authorities had been involved in some way in addressing the issue of economic development. Historically this involvement had been limited to carrying out statutory duties which impinged on business – for example, planning, housing provision, services and physical infrastructure. This developed to embrace more active specific programmes including the provision of industrial estates and factories and promotional campaigns to attract companies into the area. More recently several authorities have raised funds, mostly under section 137 of the 1972 Local Government Act (section 83 in Scotland) to provide a budget specifically for investment and loans to local firms. Moving beyond this, a few authorities have developed local strategies involving formalized objectives and a set of programmes. These plans may be linked to wider political aims, specifically with the themes of 'democracy', 'control' and 'planning'. For example, Sheffield City Council has built up an economic development department which as well as providing data and support on the local economy to trades unionists has become the centre of the council's support for 'socially useful' production and co-operative enterprise.

In Scotland several local authorities have supported the concept of community business. Strathclyde Region, in conjunction with several district councils and other agencies including the Scottish Development Agency, has set up Strathclyde Community Business specifically to support this form of enterprise through the provision of management and business advice, training, funding and promotion.

The most radical initiatives from the left-wing perspective have sought to link intervention at the micro or enterprise level with an overall strategy for the economic development of the area, including objectives for sector-wide planning. The West Midlands, West Yorkshire and Greater London (GLC) councils were examples of these authorities.

Thus, at a general level there has been a significant growth in the involvement and investment of local authorities in the field of economic development. Coulson's (1986) data calculated that the total resources directed by local authorities in England and Wales to local economic development and promotion in 1985–6 was £255.5 million revenue and £154.1 million capital (this excluded the GLC). English and Welsh authorities employed over 2,400 people on economic development functions. Using surveys of local authorities in 1984, Coulson shows that the most significant activities in terms of local authority involvement were provision of premises (65 per cent) and land registries (65 per cent), advice on location (65 per cent) and general business advice (47 per cent). The lowest areas of involvement were in the provision of equity finance (6.5 per cent) and wages subsidies (10 per cent).

The narrowing of policy

Urban policy has become concerned with economic problems and employment. The 1977 White Paper on the inner cities (Department of the Environment, 1977) provided the basis for comprehensive area projects involving all relevant public agencies addressing social, environmental and economic issues. However, this comprehensive approach based on public-sector intervention has progressively been replaced in the 1980s by a much narrower focus on economic development, in particular the encouragement of small businesses, and on projects managed by the private sector through instruments such as enterprise trusts. Urban policy has shifted from a social redistributive concern towards a modified market model (Moore and Booth, 1986a).

The spatial focus of policy has also shifted. Initially from the 1930s through the 1970s the problem was seen primarily as one of regional imbalance. However, at the same time during the 1940s and 1950s there was a concern with creating growth points within regions around New Towns. This had an effect on the urban core as businesses and the economically active population moved out, leaving behind a highly dependent population supported by an ever declining fiscal base. From the 1970s the inner cities became the focus of policy to the extent that in Clydeside the decision to build another New Town at Stonehouse was cancelled, and resources were concentrated on Glasgow's East End.

Regional policy proved inadequate largely because the national economy suffered major decline. Policy options were thus sought at different spatial levels. The Conservative governments of the 1980s have changed the emphasis within regional policy, so that it has become more narrowly defined spatially and more restrictive financially, on the grounds that previous policy was too generalized and therefore not cost-effective in terms of creating jobs (Hasluck, 1987).

While significant attention has thus been given to inner-city areas during the last ten years, it is the peripheral housing estates at the edge of this conurbation which remain marginal in terms of physical location, economic activity and political priority (CES, 1984; McGregor and Mather, 1986; Moore and Booth, 1986a). Policy-makers are still searching for an effective response to the problems of these areas.

The role of the private sector has also changed significantly from one of client to one of policy participant and manager of projects. As we argue in our studies of individual partnership initiatives, however, it would be misleading to view these trends as 'privatization', since they depend on public funding and on the active involvement of local authorities. Alternative approaches 'imposing' partnership, through UDCs, may bypass local authorities but still depend on central government finance.

Another dimension to local economic regeneration is the role of regional development agencies in Scotland and Wales. In England the absence of such regional agencies led the metropolitan country councils to develop their own alternative strategies and instruments such as the enterprise boards.

Policy models and levels of response

We can conceive of local economic policy as being concerned with three levels of economic activity: the spatial or area level, the level of the enterprise or firms and the individual as an economic actor. Each of the alternative perspectives outlined earlier will propose different responses and instruments at each of these levels. Figure 2.1 illustrates these alternatives.

We have argued that in Scotland the policies of local authorities have been influenced by the presence of the Scottish Development Agency (SDA), so that radical local initiatives have been 'crowded out' as authorities have looked to work with the SDA and accepted

POLICY MODEL

LEVEL	Liberal market	Modified market	Socialized
Area	Enterprise Zones Freeing constraints	UDCs, SDA – targeted intervention working with private sector	Enterprise boards Community-based economic development
Enterprise	Deregulation	Enterprise trusts – programmes for encouraging new firms	Planning agreements Encouraging co-ops and community businesses
Individual	Mobility Encouraging the entrepreneur	Retraining	Improving collective control of labour over capital Stimulating involvement in alternative forms of economic enterprise

Figure 2.1 Competing models and levels of intervention in the local economy.

the terms of its aid, even when it leads to contradictions with stated policy objectives (Moore and Booth, 1986a). In England radical socialist local authorities presented a challenge at an ideological level to central government strategies (Duncan and Godwin, 1985). The problem for them was in translating ideology into practice. The enterprise boards could not fulfil the more radical hopes and objectives of some of their supporters (Eisenschitz and North, 1986).

Responses to specific issues can be markedly different between the three competing perspectives. For example, the approach of the modified market model to training would place this as a major component of the fight against structural unemployment. The rapid expansion of MSC programmes reflects the fact that the private sector itself is unlikely to meet national training needs. It has long been a criticism of UK industry that it lags a long way behind continental European countries in investing in training (MSC/NEDO, 1984 and 1985; MSC 1986). The liberal market approach would see training largely as a matter for individuals and companies. In practice this position is unrealistic. The Conservative government has seen training through the MSC as a major plank of its economic regeneration strategy. However, its aim is to see the private sector taking more responsibility for the form and direction of training. Hence the growing emphasis within the YTS on the Mode A employer-based schemes as opposed to Mode B community-based schemes. The aboliton of several Industrial Training Boards is another way in which training in individual sectors is being returned to voluntary private arrangements. Most recently the idea of City Technology Colleges has been developed whereby private firms in partnership with central government set up colleges outside local authority control. These colleges are designed to run curricula to meet the educational needs of industry.

The socialized approach would see training as one component of a strategy to combat deskilling and to give individuals more control over their economic destiny. Community-based training initiatives have been pioneered by authorities such as the West Midlands through the council and, since its abolition, by the Enterprise Board.

Local authority capacity

The capacity of local authorities to undertake economic development programmes depends on legal powers and available resources (financial and human). Economic development is not a statutory function of local authorities, although a range of their statutory responsibilities such as planning, infrastructure and education clearly impinge on business. Permissive legislation has enabled local authorities to build factories and provide limited assistance, mainly in the form of grants or loans for physical developments by firms. The 1972 Local Government Act under section 137 allowed local authorities to spend up to the product of a 2p rate on any policy deemed to be of general interest to their area. The 1982 Local Government (Miscellaneous Provisions) Act explicitly included expenditure on economic initiatives as legitimate under the 2p rate product. The Inner Urban Areas Act of 1978 gave designated authorities additional powers for assisting industrial development and co-operatives. Several local authorities have also sought powers through local Acts.

Organizational change within local government to take account of this activity varies. Many authorities continue to locate economic development in planning departments, reflecting the historical bias towards factory building and environmental improvements. Others have adapted their internal organization to provide a specific focus for economic development – a section within planning or the chief executive's department, often containing a research and data-gathering capacity and acting as co-ordinator for the involvement of functional departments. A few authorities have produced policy statements and economic development plans outlining their objectives and range of programmes – for example, Glasgow, Sheffield and the GLC.

The most far-reaching change has been the setting up of enterprise boards accountable to the local authority but outside the conventional departmental structure. This has extended the organizational capacity of authorities to plan and to intervene in the local economy by providing a strategic focus for policy, specific funds for programmes and specialist staff, including people from outside local government. Other authorities have preferred to work in partnership with established agencies, for example in Scotland with the SDA, or jointly with other local authorities, such as the Lanarkshire Industrial Field Executive (Moore and Booth, 1986b), or increasingly with the private sector through enterprise trusts. This partnership approach can have a significant impact on how local authorities define policy and develop responses. For example, Strathclyde Regional Council drew up a list of locations for a programme of Joint Economic Initiatives with the SDA, and the way this list was finally prepared indicated a powerful implicit influence by the SDA. Areas that had been identified on the original list as justifying JEI status on the basis of economic and social need (deprivation, unemployment, physical dereliction) were excluded from the final list because they lacked what were termed the 'appropriate development opportunity factors' (Moore and Booth, 1986a, p. 378).

Direct expenditure on economic development by local authorities is fairly marginal. For example, Glasgow District Council's identified expenditure under its Economic Development Plan for 1985 showed proposals to spend nearly £1 million revenue and £7.3 million capital, with further commitments of around £2.5 million. In contrast, the housing revenue account envisaged expenditure of £150 million and capital expenditure of £60 million. This significant amount of money committed to statutory services has led to the notion of 'bending' mainline programmes to influence the economic development of localities (Jolliffe, 1984); but the problem is that the bulk of such expenditure is committed to meeting statutory duties, and there is increasingly little scope for manoeuvre. There is also the difficulty in changing the attitudes of functional service departments with entrenched 'professionalism' to co-ordinate with other council objectives. At the same time, the impact of, say, house building and rehabilitation on the local economy, both through the employment of building workers and through attracting new residents to an area, is potentially significant (Maclennan, 1987; Maclennan, Munro and Lamont, 1987).

Young and Mills (1983) identified the internal problem of getting policy actors to change their perceptions in response to the external environment and argued that 'policy entrepreneurs', often middle-level officials within the authority, had to challenge the power of the status quo at the senior levels in order to secure change. Some local authorities will be ideologically opposed to intervention in the local economy as a function of the authority. Others will be pragmatically opposed on the grounds that local authorities have limited powers and resources and that economic development is peripheral to their main concerns. Some authorities have a level of commitment but are sceptical as to its value outside displaying a political statement of concern about unemployment.

In a study of Clydeside local authorities Moore and Booth (1986b) identified four possible responses influenced by two variables. The first variable was the political and administrative power to induce change, i.e. the internal conflict between 'policy entrepreneurs' and those committed to the status quo. The second variable was responsiveness to the external environment. These two variables interacted to produce four model responses.

Those authorities with a low responsiveness to their external environment and a low capacity for internal change were described as *functionalist*, retaining the traditional departmental structure of organization and integrating any economic development activities into these patterns. Most of the authorities under this response located their economic development functions within their planning depart-ments. Those authorities with high internal capacity for change but low responsiveness to the external environment were committed to a *co-ordination* model of response. They would work with other agencies—the SDA, for example—which would take the lead in setting the policy agenda, but were prepared to make internal organizational changes in order to carry out their part of any agreement. Where there was a low capacity for change internally but a high responsiveness externally the authority would *externalize* its commitment by putting resources (mainly money but also seconded staff) into external agencies, for example enterprise trusts. This externalization model was different from the co-ordination approach because it involved no organizational change within the authority. It was simply a transfer of resources to an external agency, with a commitment by the agency to some form of accountability to the authority. Finally, where there was a high response to the environment and a high capacity for change internally this led to a *reorganization* model. The setting up of enterprise boards was one form of reorganization which emphasized the creation of a free-standing agency accountable to the authority. Another reorganization approach was the establishing of new units or departments within the council to manage and co-ordinate economic development policy.

Programmes

In terms of the actual programmes local authorities are carrying out, the overwhelming emphasis is on supply-side factors, either 'hardware' such as premises or 'software' such as finance and training schemes. Local authorities have very limited influence over the level of demand in the economy, although it is perhaps easy to underestimate their power in this respect. Authorities are major contractors and purchasers of goods and services and can use this commercial buying power to benefit local businesses through such means as contract preference. For example, Bennington (1986) looked at the local economic power of Sheffield City Council. It spent £84 million on construction, repair work and building-related activity. Of this about 75 per cent was estimated to go to local firms. The authority purchased goods to the value of £80 million of which £20 million went to local firms. It was the largest employer in the city, with 32,000 workers, which made it five times bigger than the city's largest private-sector employer.

Other ways in which authorities might indirectly seek to influence demand is to link their intervention at the level of the firm to some strategic conception of sector-wide development of an industry – for example, the concepts of 'industrial villages', technology networks or collective marketing and promotion.

The other major focus of local authority economic development work is small firms. This is not surprising. The opportunities to influence capital or business clearly lie more with smaller local enterprises than with large externally owned companies with local branch plants. It is quite clear from reading through the GLC's *Industrial Strategy* (1985) that the formulation of sector strategies is far more advanced in sectors dominated by small indigenous enterprises, such as textiles, than in sectors dominated by multinationals, for example the motor industry. Simply looking at the type of firm helped by enterprise boards confirms this impression. The West Midlands board took an explicit policy decision to focus its resources for investment in medium-sized indigenous manufacturing companies requiring modernization in order to become competitive. The West Yorkshire Board has concentrated on smaller local firms which suffer an 'equity gap' because of the lack of attention given to them by London-based financial institutions. Sheffield City Council has emphasized support for co-operatives. However, it is not only the size of the firm that influences enterprise boards and local authority strategy; but in practice they are constrained by the willingness of firms to approach them. This is particularly the case for authorities attempting to link aid with planning agreements and controls over management autonomy. It is unlikely that commercially successful firms requiring capital investment will approach enterprise boards if they perceive that this would mean the imposition of conditions on how they operate. Local authorities may then be left with firms in difficulty and with no alternative sources of funding, which have little option but to accept the terms of the planning agreement. In this context the concept of 'restructuring for labour' becomes somewhat threadbare. As Eisenschitz and North (1986) argue, planning agreements for such firms either worsen their commercial viability by imposing additional non-market costs and controls on performance, or in fact increase the rate of exploitation of the workers by restructuring on the terms of the market. The GLC's *Industrial Strategy* described the Greater London Enterprise Board (GLEB) as operating 'in and against the market' (GLC, 1985), perhaps not fully appreciating the ambiguity and contradictions inherent in this phrase.

Impact

If the key to unemployment and economic growth lies in the level of demand in the economy, how important are local authority initiatives? Layard and Nickell (1985) estimated that 75 per cent of the increase in unemployment between 1975–9 and 1980–3 was the result of deficient demand. But as Hasluck (1987) points out, while increased demand is critical to the recovery of local economies it is in itself insufficient to cope with the problems of urban unemployment, since it may not impact on marginalized groups or areas. Indeed, demand may contribute to the restructuring of capital rather than specifically to the benefit of labour. On the other hand, the problems facing local initiatives – whether they are spatially targeted programmes from the centre, such as Urban Aid, or local authority initiatives – include the availability of resources, the *ad hoc* and fragmentary nature of such interventions and the likely result of simply displacing jobs in an enterprise or one area. Radical socialist initiatives such as enterprise boards are constrained by the problem of how to exert control over capital on terms which are radically different from the market while operating in a market capitalist economy.

The economic impact of local authority intervention is difficult to assess. External influences, competing policies at the local level and unclear policy objectives confuse any clear analysis. However, one lesson does emerge. Local authority initiatives are marginal. For example, Bennington (1986) in examining the impact of enterprise boards estimates that they have helped create or maintain in excess of 10,000 jobs at a cost per job of £5,000. He argues that this is impressive and cost-effective expenditure, but he also says that it has to be placed in context; Sheffield, for example, estimated that it has created or sustained 1,000 jobs over two years, but the rate of local job loss in 1986 was 1,000 per month. Hasluck (1987) observed that GLEB's claim of creating or saving 4,000 jobs in London had to be set against the official unemployment rate of 400,000. Of course it can be argued that without these interventions the situation could have been much worse, and that crude job figures do not take into account the multiplier effect within the local economy. However, one cannot disagree with Hasluck's conclusion that 'it has to be recognized that such radical employment initiatives on their own will not achieve any dramatic reductions in urban unemployment' (Hasluck, 1987, pp. 213–14).

Local authorities would not dispute this. What enterprise boards may end up being is another, perhaps more socially aware, form of financial investment capital, rather than promoting 'restructuring for labour' (Eisenschitz and North, 1986). Or alternatively they may be viewed in more symbolic terms as examples of what a socialized economic strategy at the local level might look like and as an ideological challenge to central government's market model. Or, as

Duncan and Godwin put it: 'It is not so much what local state institutions do but how they do it' (Duncan and Godwin, 1985, p. 244).

This constraint is recognized by Hasluck (1987) when he concludes by saying that such radical models must remain marginal in the absence of any central economic strategy of intervention and planning of the macro-economy. He calls for local strategies and instruments of intervention to be located within a national strategy, a federal model of enterprise boards.

Conclusion

Bennington (1986) raised the question of whether local authority involvement in economic development would be a passing fad or represent a long-term commitment. He concluded that the latter seemed more likely given the growth of investment and the political support for initiatives. However, he then sounded a note of caution about whether economic development would remain a 'frontier' service pioneering new forms of intervention and catalytic activity or whether it would become 'incorporated and routinized within the bureaucracy'. He warned that 'the radical interventions of today could easily become the routine employment "services" of tomorrow – local economic units operating like decentralized offices of the MSC' (Bennington, 1986, p. 21).

Bennington broadly divided local economic intervention into market-based approaches, characterizing the central Conservative government's approach, and 'new left' local authority intervention which in his view were radical initiatives. We would reject this simple dichotomy, preferring Hasluck's more complex analysis with at least three competing perspectives: liberal market, modified market and socialized market. In practice, policies become confused and ambiguous. For example, Enterprise Zones or UDCs are put forward by a liberal market government but in fact are interventions in the market either through massive financial subsidies for capital (a micro-version of regional policy) or through centrally funded agencies displacing local government responsibility for the physical and economic regeneration of designated areas. The ultimate objectives and guiding practice of these initiatives may be based on market assumptions, but they are hardly examples of deregulation or lack of state intervention. Similarly, 'radical left' interventions by local authorities face contradictions which cannot be resolved at the local level. In essence, the problem is a contradiction between the pursuit of political goals about planned socialized economic restructuring and a market economy. This leads initiatives to modify their original ideological values, pay lip-service to them, or remain consistent but marginalized.

But if these different approaches illustrate the problems confronting local economic development policies, what of the 'partnership model' of local public and private consensus, put forward by central government and supported by many local authorities (Labour, Conservative, SLD or SDP)? What of the enterprise agency? It is this type of model, which is certainly politically significant but has not been treated with sufficient independent analysis, that we examine in the following chapters.

References

Armstrong, H., and Riley, D. (1987), 'The "North–South",'controversy and Britain's regional problems', *Local Economy*, vol. 2, no. 2, August, pp. 93–107.

Begg, I., and Moore, B. (1987), 'The changing economic role of Britain's cities', in V. Hausner (ed.), *Critical Issues in Urban Economic Development*, vol. II (Oxford: Oxford University Press), pp. 44–76.

Bennington, J. (1986), 'Local economic strategies: paradigms for a planned economy?', *Local Economy*, vol. 1, no. 1, spring, pp. 7–25.

Boddy, M., and Fudge, C. (eds) (1984), *Local Socialism? Labour Councils and New Left Alternatives* (London: Macmillan).

Bulpitt, J. (1983), *Territory and Power in the United Kingdom: An Interpretation*, (Manchester: Manchester University Press).

Cambridge Econometrics (1987), *Regional Economic Prospects: Analysis and Forecasts to the Year 2,000* (Cambridge: Cambridge Econometrics).

CES (1984), *Outer Estates in Britain: A 'Framework for Action'*, Part I: A *Discussion Paper*, CES Paper No. 28 (London: CES Ltd).

Checkland, S. (1976), *The Upas Tree: Glasgow 1875–1975* (Glasgow: Glasgow University Press).

Coulson, A. (1986), *Economic Development: The Future Role and Organization of Local Government*, Functional Study No. 6 (Birmingham: Institute of Local Government Studies, University of Birmingham).

Department of Employment (1987), *Employment Gazette*, January (London: HMSO).

Department of Employment (1988), *Employment Gazette*, October (London: HMSO).

Department of the Environment (1977), *Policy for the Inner Cities*, Cmnd 6845 (London: HMSO).

Drewett, R., Goddard, K., and Spence, M. (1976), *Urban Change in Britain: 1961–71*, Working Paper No. 21 (London: Department of Geography, London School of Economics).

Duncan, S., and Godwin, M. (1985), 'The local state and economic policy: why all the fuss?', *Policy and Politics*, vol. 13, no. 3, pp. 227–53.

Eisenschitz, A., and North, D. (1986), *The London Industrial Strategy:* socialist transformation or modernizing capitalism?', *International Journal of Urban and Regional Research*, vol. 10, no. 3, pp. 419–39.

Fothergill, S., and Gudgin, G. (1982), *Unequal Growth, Urban and Regional Employment Changes in the UK* (London: Heinemann Educational).

Greater London Council (1985), *The London Industrial Strategy* (London: GLC).

Green, A. (1985), 'Unemployment duration in the recession: the local labour market area scale', *Regional Studies*, vol. 19, no. 2, pp. 111–29.

Hasluck, C. (1987), *Urban Unemployment: Local Labour Markets and Employment Initiatives* (London: Longmans).

Hausner, V., and Robson, B. (1986), *Changing Cities*, revised edn (London: Economic and Social Research Council).

Jolliffe, C. (1984), *Bending Mainline Programmes: The Utilization of Main Programmes for Urban Regeneration*, Working Paper No. 8, The Inner City in Context: Clydeside Case Study (Glasgow: Economic and Social Research Council and Department of Social and Economic Research, University of Glasgow).

Layard, P., and Nickell, S. (1985), 'The causes of British unemployment', *National Institute Economic Review*, no. 11, February.

Lever, W., and Mather, F. (1986), 'The changing structure of business and employment in the conurbation', in W. Lever and C. Moore (eds), *The City in Transition: Policies and Agencies for the Economic Regeneration of Clydeside* (Oxford: Oxford University Press), pp. 1–21.

McArthur, A. (1987), 'Jobs and incomes', in D. Donnison and A. Middleton (eds), *Regenerating the Inner City: Glasgow's Experience* (London: Routledge & Kegan Paul), pp. 72–92.

McGregor, A., and Mather, F. (1986), 'Developments in Glasgow's labour market', in W. Lever and C. Moore (eds), *The City in Transition: Policies and Agencies for the Economic Regeneration of Clydeside* (Oxford: Oxford University Press), pp. 22–43.

Maclennan, D. (1987), 'Rehabilitating older housing', in D. Donnison and A. Middleton (eds), *Regenerating the Inner City: Glasgow's Experience* (London: Routledge & Kegan Paul), pp. 117–34.

Maclennan, D., Munro, M., and Lamont, D. (1987), 'New owner-occupied housing', in D. Donnison and A. Middleton (eds), *Regenerating the Inner City: Glasgow's Experience* (London: Routledge & Kegan Paul), pp. 131–51.

Maclennan, D., and Parr, J. (eds) (1979), *Regional Policy: Past Experiences and New Directions* (Oxford: Martin Robertson).

Manpower Services Commission/National Economic Development Office (1984), *Competence and Competition* (London: Institute of Manpower Studies for the MSC/NEDO).

MSC/NEDO (1985), *A Challenge to Complacency* (London: Coopers & Lybrand for the MSC/NEDO).

MSC (1986), *Small Firms Survey* (Sheffield: MSC).

Moore, C., and Booth, S. (1986a), 'Urban policy contradictions: the market versus redistributive approaches', *Policy and Politics*, vol. 14, no. 3, July, pp. 361–87.

Moore, C., and Booth, S. (1986b), 'The pragmatic approach: local political models of regeneration', in W. Lever and C. Moore (eds), *The City in Transition: Policies and Agencies for the Economic Regeneration of Clydeside*, (Oxford: Oxford University Press), pp. 92–106.

Naughtie, J. (1986), 'DTI paints gloomy picture of regional decay and collapse', *Guardian*, 21 October.

North of England County Councils Association (1986), *Review of Change 1977–1985: The State of the Region Report 1985* (Newcastle: NECCA).

Parkinson, M. (1986), *Liverpool on the Brink: One City's Struggle against Government Cuts* (Hermitage, Berks: Policy Journals).

Spencer, K., Taylor, A., Smith, B., Mawson, J., Flynn, N., and Battey, R. (1986), *Crisis in the Industrial Heartland: A Study of the West Midlands* (Oxford: Oxford University Press).

Stoker, G. (1988), *The Politics of Local Government* (Basingstoke: Macmillan Education).

Wolman, H. (1987), 'Urban economic performance: a comparative analysis', in V. Hausner (ed.), *Critical Issues in Urban Economic Development*, Vol. II (Oxford: Oxford University Press), pp. 9–43.

Young, K., and Mills, L. (1983), *Managing the Post-Industrial City* (London: Heinemann Educational).

3 Local responses: the organisational network

Introduction: varieties of partnership

We have seen at the national level the development of new forms of co-operation between the public and private sectors in the key policy areas of urban policy and economic regeneration. There has been a fundamental shift away from large-scale public-sector-based projects like the Inner-City Partnerships to joint public–private schemes and a tighter focus on business development (Moore and Booth, 1986a). The rise of the corporate responsibility movement through umbrella organizations like Business in the Community (BIC) has provided a focus for private-sector entry into these policy arenas as a formulator and implementor of programmes at the local level. Richardson (1983) has described the emergence of this movement from the late 1970s in the UK, identifying the influence of US experience as well as national political and social factors. Corporate responsibility has moved from philanthropy and 'good citizenship' to a third stage which reflects the growing political and social demands made by society on business. Corporations have developed policy and strategies to cope with what Thomas (1977) calls the 'negotiated environment'. It is this third level which many US writers have osberved as being of crucial significance in the modern corporation (Vogel and Bradshaw, 1980). It is no longer acceptable for the corporation just to focus on the market as the criteria of its social performance. One specific organisational manifestation of this is the growth of political or public affairs units in big companies (Grant, 1981 and 1987).

A growing dimension of corporate affairs units is in guiding company involvement in local employment initiatives. The explosion of such initiatives is not confined to the UK but can be observed as a European phenomenon (Centre for Employment Initiatives, 1982; Todd, 1984). Not all companies are equally involved in or committed to the notion of investing in local economic or employment projects. As part of our research we carried out a survey of over one hundred major UK companies in the manufacturing and financial services sectors (Moore, Richardson and Moon, 1985). This found a variety of responses, which we can categorize as:

(1) *Traditional*, where the company made no distinction between local economic involvement and being a large employer and thus had no explicit corporate policy outside its commercial activities.

(2) *Narrow* definition, where the company thought in terms of progressive internal policies on matters such as health and safety, industrial relations, or equal opportunities.

(3) *Fragmented* response, where the company did have some involvement at local plant level but lacked any concerted central thrust or policy framework.

(4) *Concerted internalized* response, primarily characterized by a major involvement in training schemes like YTS or intensive counselling programmes for redundant workers.

(5) *Concerted externalized*, which represented the highest level of involvement. This is where companies sponsored community-based projects which had no direct commercial or organizational benefit for themselves. Such companies can be identified by their explicit policy statements, organizational responsibility and level of resources committed to projects.

At the time of the survey we found most of the responses falling into the 'fragmented' category, confirming previous research (Dichlin, 1983). BIC was established to encourage more companies to move into the 'concerted externalized' category. While the USA was held up as a model of active corporate responsibility, there were examples nearer home. In particular, Pilkington was the pioneer of the local enterprise trust movement in the UK through its sponsorship of the St Helens Trust (see below).

Before BIC, the Confederation of British Industry (CBI) had set up a Special Programmes Unit (SPU), at the request of the government, to promote business participation in MSC schemes, especially the new YTS. It expanded its activities to examine other ways in which companies could become involved in local economic projects and mounted a series of town studies or Community Action Programmes (CAPs). These were studies of selected localities in order to analyse, in conjunction with local authorities and other organizations, the economic and employment problems of the area, and to explore ways in which the public and private sectors could come together to address these problems. BIC, which emerged out of a special conference convened by Tom King, Secretary of State for the Environment, at Sunningdale in 1981, brought together not only business interests but the TUC, the voluntary sector and local government. It concerned itself primarily with encouraging local enterprise trusts (ETs). In October 1984 the SPU and BIC merged under the BIC umbrella. A similar organization was established in Scotland (ScotBIC) to act as the central co-ordinating body for the growing ET movement there. This organization was actively supported by the government's main economic development agency in Scotland, the Scottish Development Agency (SDA), which saw ETs as a way of extending its own influence in local economic development (Moore and Booth, 1986b).

High-profile partnership between the public and private sectors at national level needs to be seen in the context of what is happening on the ground locally, since this is the rationale for encouraging the whole ET movement. Abraham (1974) has categorized the various roles of central government in its relationship to business. These roles include government as facilitator and promoter and as director and controller. Similarly, at local level there is a growing interaction between government and business as local authorities seek to extend their involvement in economic development (Young and Mills, 1983; Chandler and Lawless, 1985). We can describe the most significant relationships in terms of four basic models:

(1) Local authority as *customer* of the private sector, for example in awarding contracts and purchasing goods and services. This relationship, which is primarily a commercial or market relationship, has become increasingly politicized with the drive by central government to privatize public services, including those traditionally undertaken by local authorities, for example refuse collection, and by certain authorities seeking to use their purchasing power to secure certain political objectives – for example, employment of ethnic minorities or union recognition.

(2) Local authority as *subsidizer* by providing a range of services and facilities which may be partly done on a commercial basis, partly viewed as collective provision paid for by the rates and partly sub-sidized in order to generate private-sector activity. Examples of such provision would include building and renting factories and workshops, business advisory services and loans and grants schemes.

(3) Local authority as *regulator* through its statutory responsibilities as a planning and development control agency and for a variety of policy areas – for example, consumer protection, health and safety and the environment.

(4) Local authority as *partner*, where it joins with the private sector in the development of projects – for example, building factories, housing, or commercial properties. This form of partnership has been greatly encouraged by central government through mechanisms like the Urban Development Grant (UDG) (Boyle, 1985).

It is this fourth model which concerns this study. But the term 'partnership' obscures a diversity of organizational structures and relationships. A dominant characteristic of urban policy partnerships has been their limited *ad hoc* project basis. Enterprise trusts, however, represent potentially a new stage of local partnership, seeking to go beyond one-off development projects to address strategic issues of long-term economic development and management of transition. This generates new policy communities or networks. Enterprise trusts do not represent a simple 'privatization' of public policy in the sense of parcelling out responsibilities from the public to the private sector. Rather they are yet another arena for the intermeshing of public and private, identified by Hague, McKenzie and Barker (1975) as 'the institutions of compromise'. It is to these institutions that we now turn.

Neath: the new model partnership

Enormous political capital has been invested in the enterprise trust movement as the leading edge of the new public–private partnerships set up in the last decade to tackle the problems of local economic collapse. They are seen as a critical part of the strategy to create an 'enterprise culture' in areas traditionally dependent on employment in large manufacturing plants. The Neath Development Partnership (NDP) has been held up as a model of this joint initiative and provided the central empirical focus of our research.

Planning and mobilization

The origins of NDP can be traced to the recommendations of the Neath Town Study of August 1981. This was sponsored by the newspaper and leisure conglomerate, the International Thomson Organization (ITO), which, through its subsidiary, Thomson Newspapers, owned the local evening and regional daily news-papers. ITO was an active supporter of the CBI's Special Programmes Units.

The Neath study team comprised representatives from Thom-son's, Neath Borough Council (NBC) (one of whose councillors had been seconded by his employer, Metal Box, to the SPU) and PA Management Consultants. The choice of Neath by these corporate sponsors was thus clearly influenced by personal and corporate linkages. The report examined recent trends in the local economy, especially relating to employment, and made several recommenda-tions for action. In order to structure and co-ordinate a local response to the problems identified, the study recommended the creation of a 'development partnership' bringing together the local authority, industry and trades unions. ITO would supply secondees to head up this new body.

Organizaton and structure

NDP was set up as a company limited by guarantee without share capital. It is a registered enterprise agency, which means that sponsors can offset their contributions against tax. The original overall structure of the organization is depicted in Figure 3.1.

The Board of Directors comprises individuals from the agency's sponsors plus invited individuals from important interests like the Welsh Development Agency (WDA). Membership was kept deliberately small. The guiding philosophy was that only interests who could positively 'bring something to the picnic', in the form either of money or of support in kind, should be invited. The involvement of local politicians and trades unionists was significant in terms of extending local contacts, creating legitimacy and securing community support.

Detailed operational control of NDP's activities was exercised through a series of subcommittees and subsidiary agencies and the full-time staff. As the activities of NDP grew, so the organization had to adapt to meet the demands of effective management. Several staff were employed on short-term contracts, principally through Urban Aid funding.

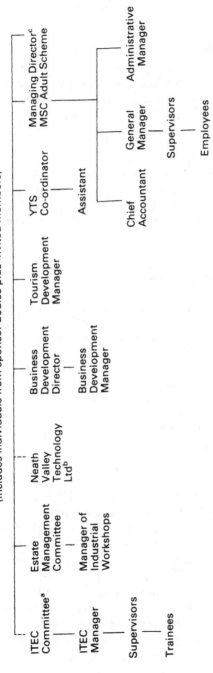

Chairman

Board of Directors
(includes individuals from sponsor bodies plus invited members)

ITEC Committee[a]

Estate Management Committee

Neath Valley Technology Ltd[b]

Business Development Director

Tourism Development Manager

YTS Co-ordinator

Managing Director[c] MSC Adult Scheme

ITEC Manager

Manager of Industrial Workshops

Business Developiopment Manager

Assistant

Supervisors

Trainees

Chief Accountant

General Manager

Administrative Manager

Supervisors

Employees

Notes:

—— Direct accountability to main board

- - - - Indirect accountability

a   ITEC constituted as company limited by guarantee. Board of Directors includes non-Partnership members. Board as ITEC Committee.

b   NVT Ltd constituted as company limited by guarantee.

c   Managing Director MSC is member of Partnership Board.

Figure 3.1   Neath Development Partnership outline structure.

Resourcing

Funding and support in kind for NDP can be divided into two main categories: core funding, covering staffing, administrative and running costs; and project funding, supporting specific operational activities. In addition, we can distinguish between sources of funds on a public–private dichotomy. The resourcing of NDP can thus be presented in the form of a matrix as shown in Figure 3.2.

		Activity — Project	Activity — Core
Source:	Public	Urban Aid, EEC, WDA, Local authorities – capital funding Revenue funding – feasibility studies, business counselling	Neath Borough Council (£45,000 over 3 years)
	Private	Secondments and access to management expertise Facilities, e.g. premises, disused sites Commissioning reports NCB business development fund BP business development fund	Metal Box ⎫ ITO ⎬ Total annual grant of £15,000 BP ⎭ NCB (Enterprise) funds for Business Development Manager (£45,000 over 3 years) ITO secondments

Figure 3.2   Resourcing the Partnership.

In analyzing the motives for private-sector commitment it is significant that both British Petroleum and Metal Box had major local branch plants which had been undergoing extensive rationalization. This stimulated their interest in doing something positive (and being seen to be so doing) to relieve the consequences on the community of their own commercial decisions. In April 1984 BP announced plans to cut the workforce at its Llandarcy refinery by 750, or 50 per cent, over eighteen months. Following this decision, BP increased its commitment to local economic projects by seconding extra staff and releasing surplus land for development and by creating a subsidzed loans fund for new small firms. This commitment was formalized and extended in 1987 when BP formed a separate company to utilize the redundant Llandarcy site for redevelopment and take over the administration of the small business loans fund. It was reported that BP was investing £1 million in the new company with the objective of securing a further £3 million from public and private sources (BIC, 1987).

Despite these various inputs from the private sector, one of the great myths about enterprise agencies is that they are overwhelmingly resourced by companies, with public agencies making only a marginal topping-up contribution. This image is enhanced by the explicit policy guidelines of government departments concerning support for enterprise agencies. For example, the Welsh Office, which supported designated agencies mainly through its Urban Aid budget, gave grants for core funding to act as pump-priming money restricted to a period of three years. The objective was that after this period agencies would be self-supporting. Responses by the Welsh Office to specific requests for such funding were on the basis of the level of private-sector commitment.

However, in the case of Neath – and as we will show, in this sense it is not unusual – input from the public sector towards running costs equals or even exceeds private sponsorship, certainly in cash terms. For example, NDP received a grant of £45,000 over the first three years from Neath Council towards core funding, which equalled the combined private-sector contribution. It is more difficult to quantify other private-sector support, particularly secondments, but it is clear that Neath Council contributed significantly to core funding, and more importantly the public sector was a major source of funds for project expenditure. In 1986 the House of Commons Select Committee on Welsh Affairs investigated the impact of enterprise agencies on job creation. Funding for NDP between 1981 and 1987 totalled £1.147 million, of which £687,000 was from public-sector sources (including British Steel and British Coal job-creation subsidiaries) and £460,000 from the private sector. During the same period other economic development expenditure by the public sector totalled £13.6 million. This figure included a contribution from the MSC, through Community Programme and YTS, of over £7 million, and investment by the local authority, the Welsh Office and the European Regional Development Fund (Welsh Committee, 1986).

The easiest way to obtain a broad picture of the project resourcing of NDP is to breakdown its different areas of activity. This is presented in Table 3.1. Where expenditure can be quantified, it clearly shows that, at least in the short to medium term, the public sector was playing the lead role. Whether one sees this as 'pump-priming' or 'leverage' designed to attract much more significant private-sector investment, as in the Special Project concept (see Chapter 4), does not detract from the importance of the public purse in one form or another providing substantial amounts of money. Even in the longer term one can see the importance of public resourcing not simply in maintenance terms, but in further capital projects. For example, in the provision of industrial land by far the most significant portion is within public control. Of the 120 hectares of zoned land in Neath in 1985, 110 hectares was in public owernship, of which 68 hectares was owned by West Glamorgan County Council.

This high level of dependence on public funding was justified on the grounds that it was necessary in order to make projects attractive for private investment. In some proposals the need for public funding was much greater in the initial stages – for example, tourism, where the envisaged ratio of public to private investment was 50:50, as against urban renewal, where it was 30:70. However, the public-sector commitment was clearly subject to constraints due to spending cuts. This raised hard questions regarding priorities within public agencies, calling into doubt support for ambitious proposals like the Special Project in its original form.

Roles and relationships

NDP as a local response to unemployment owed much of its initial impetus to external forces. The leadership and support of major corporate interests with a stake in the local economy through branch plants were critically allied to the commitment of key local policy actors. The ease with which the private and public sectors were joined together can be explained by the local policy vacuum or space which existed before NDP. Neath Council had no developed economic policy or organizational capacity to address the issue of employment decline. It had established an industry committee and was spending about £225,000 on industrial sites and £4,000 on promotion. A report observed that this resource commitment bore 'little relationship to the task that needs doing in the future' (ITO, 1983). The authority, however, felt that it had adequate capacity and skills which it could deploy to assist economic development within the limited resources and powers available without engaging in major internal reorganiza-tion. Councillors and officials had a traditionalist attitude to the responsibilities of the authority. Essentially, the council's contribu-tion to economic development lay in bricks and mortar, providing

Table 3.1   NDP (resources profile (up to 1985)

Project	Source	Support
Provision of premises	NBC MSC ERDF Urban Aid[a]	} £800,000 to £1m.
Business counselling	WDA	Business counsellor for 2 days per week
Financial support	BP NCB (E)	Loans fund – unspecified Loans fund – NDP designated agency
Tourism	Private sector investment Public sector	£1m. to £5m.[b] £0.75m.
Special Project[c]	Public sector (NCB; Urban Aid, WDA, MSC, WTB) Private sector investment	£7.4m. £12.3m.
Youth training – ITEC	Private sector MSC, YTS, grant DTI grant – capital equipment NBC	Premises and management, trainees fees and contribution to overheads { £75,000 over 3 years { £50,000 for regional ITEC £80,000 over 3 years
Youth training – YTS	MSC	£200,000 per annum
Job creation – CP	MSC NDP Urban Aid	£1.3m. £30,000 £40,000

[a] Urban Aid funding is 75% central government and 25% local authority contribution.
[b] On the basis of committed and planning investment identified in the Tourism Development Report (1984).
[c] The Special Project was a comprehensive co-ordinated package of proposals, including urban renewal and tourism-related projects, put together by NDP in a bid for WDA support. These figures relate to the total proposed spend and not to specific commitments or actual expenditure incurred at the time of the proposal.

the infrastructure of sites and premises, and in controlling the physical planning framework.

In Young and Mill's terms the 'policy entrepreneurs' within the authority had not successfully placed economic issues on the policy agenda (Young and Mills, 1983). At the same time, there was ample evidence elsewhere of local authorities becoming extensively involved in this issue (Chandler and Lawless, 1985), although the specific organizational form of this involvement varied (Moore and Booth, 1986c).

The other critical dimension in Neath, however, was the high degree of political stability. The council was a traditionalist Labour-controlled authority. Together these two factors of policy *space* and political *stability* provided an opportunity for the 'policy entrepreneurs' within the local authority in alliance with outside forces to colonize the policy issue and mobilize support. For the Partnership to emerge as the central agency of local economic development policy there had to be a policy gap which it could fill. At the same time, the local authority had to be prepared to 'externalize' its response to this issue by working with and through another agency, albeit one over which it had considerable influence. This externalization had attractions for the authority in enabling it to extend its capacity and potential influence on economic development without demanding major internal restructuring. However, this approach also involved ceding some control over policy-making and stretching established lines of accountability.

The Partnership emerged essentially as a policy entrepreneur. It acted as a catalyst for new ideas and as a managing agent for delivering a range of special programmes. Considerable effort went into packaging schemes and bargaining with a variety of funding bodies for resources. As the Partnership became established in the local policy community it evolved into a second stage of organizational development which placed increasing emphasis on the management of substantive activities and development of new trading opportunities. The Enterprise Trust began to give way to the economic development company.

The Partnership has to be understood as both a *structure* and a *process*. The structural dimension involved a distinctive organizational entity called the Neath Development Partnership sponsored by several public and private bodies. It had its own legal identity, office and staff. As a process the whole concept of partnership which NDP embodied was about bringing together all these different actors in order to co-ordinate resources and responsibilities and to create policy consensus.

The local authority provided financial support and political legitimacy for the Partnership, while it in return provided a focus of expertise and skills and access to private-sector resources. There was a mutual commitment, although not necessarily complete harmony between the two. The Partnership was launched as a statement of private-sector commitment supported by the local authority. It remained open for either side to pull out. This would have raised political, resource and organizational issues for the council. The investment of political capital, as well as financial resources, into the Partnership implied an acknowledgement that it was the most effective instrument open to the authority. It had the important additional advantage of avoiding internal organizational change. This did not mean that relationships would remain cast in stone for all time, but it did mean that change involved a series of chain reactions and raised a number of difficult questions. Once an issue has become accepted as a legitimate part of the policy agenda it is increasingly difficult to move it off that agenda. At the same time there were tensions between the Partnership and the local authority around the issue of accountability. The balance between the need for public control and operational flexibility is a difficult one to strike, as the literature on 'Quangos' has shown (Hague, McKenzie and Barker, 1975; Barker, 1982).

The Partnership represented a fusion not only of skills, but of different policy and management styles and cultures. Tension was never likely to be far below the surface, particularly where a new agency was brought into existence which in some ways encroached on the established spatial and functional territories of other actors.

Internal dynamics

Personalities were a critical factor in an understanding of the operational style of the Partnership. The key individuals comprised a mix of outsiders from senior management in the sponsoring companies and a local community activist with access to several critical political and local networks, thereby acting as the local facilitator and broker. This dependence on individuals proved to be something of a destabilizing factor in the longer term because of the level of personal commitment demanded. The attraction of dynamic high-profile individuals was important during the early developmental stages for the agency to become established and known and to stimulate fresh policy ideas. Over the longer term the need for a clear managerial structure and processes capable of controlling projects assumed significance. Different skills were required for these different stages. Innovative individuals are not necessarily good managers. A recognized need for more routinization was agreed. At the same time, the Partnership sought to avoid over-bureaucratization. There were clearly shifts in operational style as changes in senior personnel occurred. This was reflected, for example, in the tourism strategy (see Chapter 4). Regular corporate team meetings were introduced to facilitate better internal information and contact. The Community Programme management team was strengthened. One general lesson from the Partnership's experience is that, while individuals are clearly important in small-scale organizations, an overdependence on one or two people is unhealthy for the long-term welfare of the enterprise, and of the individuals concerned.

Summary

NDP represented an attempt to move beyond *ad hoc* project-based partnership between the public and private sectors, which characterizes most urban policy initiatives in the UK. It was concerned with adopting a more strategic conception of local development. As such, NDP does not easily fit in with notions of the 'free market' approach to economic policy or with 'privatization' of public responsibilities. It was more about bringing private-sector resources into the public policy domain, thereby influencing the output of the public decision-making process. Its impacts, and importance, are as much political as economic. At one level the response represented by the Partnership is concerned with short-term crisis management, but at another it is about the strategic management of fundamental transition.

For central government there are political benefits in promoting localized responses to the unemployment crisis. The issue is exported to the local level, and solutions are narrowly defined in terms of space rather than structure. The economic decline of Neath thus becomes a question of the competitive performance of the local economy, which is tackled by improving the local supply of economic infrastructure and the generation of community-based economic activity. This neatly divorces local efforts from macro-structural problems.

There are underlying ideological shifts at work. The Neath Partnership forms part of a wider pattern in British policy-making. Several observers have noted these shifts in urban policy, with the emphasis on market solutions to public problems (Boyle and Rich, 1984; Moore and Booth, 1986a). Some have seen the makings of a new local corporatism based on alliances of local state, capital and labour (Cawson, 1985).

Whether or not one accepts this concept as a valid description, it seems clear that the impact of the Neath Partnership on policy-making raises paradoxes for central government. Essentially, it represents a form of intervention in the local economy rather than a simple assertion of the 'logic of the market'. In particular, the Partnership explodes the myth that private-sector resources can significantly replace public funding. The Partnership drew together packages of public funds from a variety of programmes in order to generate private investment. Without the availability of those public funds it is doubtful whether the Partnership could have become a meaningful agent of economic regeneration. Private-sector participation in the Partnership may have led to innovation and creative ways of using public programmes, but that does not change the fact that it was largely public money which provided the basic resources for the realization of projects. Thus, constraints on such expenditure carried implications for the Partnership. This is a paradoxical lesson for any government committed at an ideological level to market solutions.

St Helens: a company town

Origins

The St Helens Trust was the first enterprise agency established in the UK. It was set up in 1978. It is not simply this fact which has made it the subject of attention (Fazey, 1987), but the unique context in which the Trust has operated. St Helens can almost be described as a one-industry town. Glass manufacturing and related industries dominate. At one time it provided over half the town's employment. Within the industry the name of Pilkington is synonymous with glass and St Helens. Established in 1826 as the St Helens Crown Glass Company, Pilkington has grown into a multinational corporation with over one hundred subsidiaries and related companies in the UK and world-wide. Total turnover in 1984 was £1,225 million, of which 70 per cent was earned outside the UK, indicating the multinational nature of the industry and the company, which still has its headquarters in St Helens.

At its peak Pilkington employed over 20,000 people in St Helens. Currently it employs about 7,000, representing around 20 per cent of its total workforce. The genesis of the St Helens Trust can be traced to this massive rationalization programme. The position of Pilkington in St Helens is critical to understanding the relationships which have emerged between the public and private sectors.

Its high profile is not simply a matter of employment, but the history of corporate responsibility which Pilkington carries. In many ways this is reminiscent of the nineteenth-century Victorian philanthropy of Cadbury of Bournville, Rowntree of York, or Titus Oates of Saltaire. Until 1970 Pilkington was a private family-owned business, and the family still retains a major interest in the company. The importance of this was dramatically illustrated in late 1986 when there was a take-over bid by the conglomerate BTR. This led to a local alliance of town council, trades unions and the company to fight the threat to corporate autonomy.

For many years Pilkington has functioned almost as a private welfare state, providing a range of benefits and facilities for its former employees. The term 'Pilkington's pensioner' refers to the thousands of ex-employees still resident in St Helens. Thus, the concept of 'business in the community' takes on a very special meaning in St Helens.

The idea for some kind of economic development initiative grew out of an internal management training programme in 1976 designed to generate ideas on ways in which the company could respond to ease the impact on the local community of the rationalization programme brought about by changing technology and the need to diversify into overseas markets. Thus, in contrast to the experience, in Neath, the initial response was indigenous. However, Pilkington did not have a firm blueprint for some local initiative and was uncertain about the most appropriate approach to adopt. It needed some external catalyst to bring different interests together behind a concrete proposal.

The MSC's District Manpower Committee, chaired by the Managing Director of Rockware, another major glass company in the town, approached a former Pilkington manager who was at that time running a small enterprise-training workshop in London. He was asked to carry out a feasibility study based on the ideas of the internal management training exercise at Pilkington. He rejected the concepts being put forward in the proposal, which he regarded as basically a controlled training workshop which would not lead to viable self-supporting businesses. After some discussion and debate he was persuaded to take up the position on the understanding that he could develop the concept along different lines. He began to secure firm co-operation from Pilkington, the local authority, which provided him with initial office space, other local firms and the trades unions.

The Community of St Helens Trust was legally established in

September 1978. It had taken some two years from the initial Pilkington exercise to the actual launching of the Trust and had required critical outside involvement in the form of a key individual as well as commitment from local interests (for a full account of the early days and development of the Trust, see Fazey, 1987).

Organizaton and relationships

The genesis of the project helps explain how it has subsequently developed. The Trust's staff saw themselves as independent. The Board of Governors exercised general oversight but remained one step removed from the operational activities of the Trust, meeting only about four or five times each year. In comparison to NDP, the Trust's Board exerted minimum strategic control over operations. It comprised representatives of Pilkington and other local businesses, the town council and trades unions. The Director was a full-time employee, but other staff were seconded as necessary from local companies. Operational independence was seen as critical to the credibility of the initiative and reflected the desire of Pilkington to reduce the kind of paternalistic dependency relationship which had built up between company and community.

Relations between the Trust and the local authority were another key dimension to the place of the agency within St Helens. There was a high degree of contact between council officials and the Trust, which continued despite shifts at the political level in the composition and attitudes of the ruling Labour group. A more critical attitude towards the Trust emerged, reflecting criticisms about the influence of Pilkington within the town. At the same time the Trust appeared to have established itself as a long-term actor in the process of economic regeneration and as a model of its kind for other communities. As in Neath, the option was there for the local authority to withdraw its support and to assume more direct responsibility for the range of programmes offered by the Trust. The political and economic costs of withdrawal made it unlikely that the authority would completely sever its links, which in terms of direct financial support were in fact very limited. Perhaps more significantly, as in Neath, the Trust became seen as a useful means by which the local authority could achieve its own objectives in terms of economic development.

A distinctive contribution of the Trust was to have brought together various interests within the community and to have increased the co-ordination of support for business development. At the very least there was dialogue between the public and private sectors, even if there was not always agreement. This was important, because the dominance of Pilkington in St Helens did create tensions and perhaps resentment.

The Trust sparked the local authority into a more concerted effort in encouraging local economic development. Before 1979 the council's commitment was essentially part-time, based on the traditional estates and physical planning approach found in Neath. Its support for the setting up of the Trust through an Urban Aid grant helped generate changes in the council's own thinking about its role. An Economic Development Unit was created within the Chief Executive's Department, with access to a budget of about £1½ million.

While the major emphasis of Pilkington was on the Trust, the company engaged in a series of other initiatives to support diversification of the local economy. These included a venture capital fund which generated £2 million for investment in new small business, and a property development company responsible for converting old premises into new enterprise workshops. These initiatives, while significant in the context of corporate involvement in local economic initiatives, have to be set against the costs of corporate rationalization. For example, Pilkington spent about £100 million in redundancy payments. The rationalization programme produced a marked improvement in corporate commercial performance, with record pre-tax profits in 1985 of £116 million.

Summary

The significance of the St Helens model lies not simply in the fact that it was a pioneer for subsequent enterprise agencies, nor in the type of activities it undertakes, but in the unique set of relationships which characterizes the community. Partnership is dominated by the role of Pilkington, which is not simply another company or even the major private-sector employer in the town, but a social institution. In some ways its support for the Trust is designed to reduce the dependency of the community on the company. This high profile in one way makes Pilkington's commitment a critical component to any local economic initiative, but at the same time leaves it exposed to political criticism for failing to do enough. It is, however, perhaps simplistic to overstate the role of one company, even such a dominant one in the local economy as Pilkington's was in St Helens. While the company was clearly concerned with the economic and employment impact of its own rationalization, and this provided a focus for considering how it could respond, Pilkington did not create the Trust. The Trust emerged from a combination of factors, including a critical external input from an individual who played the role of broker and animator or policy entrepreneur (Fazey, 1987).

Dumbarton: from fragmentation to concerted action

Dumbarton illustrates the birth of an enterprise agency. As in Neath, it arose out of the intervention of the CBI's Special Programmes Unit through its Community Action Programme (CAP) studies. As in Neath, too, the involvement of this external agency was critical in generating a local response to the problem of economic decline. Indeed, the influence of these external forces was more marked in Dumbarton because of the lack of any significant indigenous business community. It was the SPU, through contacts with Strathclyde Regional Council, which brought together representatives from local government, business and other interests in a steering group to mount a study of the local economy in 1984. The CAP represented the first time that most of the more significant employers in the area had come together. The business community was characterized by a high degree of fragmentation, reflecting the predominance of small firms in the economy. Only three firms employed more than three hundred people, and 95 per cent of local firms employed less than ten employees (Dumbarton CAP, 1985). Thus, in contrast to Neath and St Helens, the indigenous business base for a local initiative was largely absent, and it took external intervention to create local concerted action.

Organization and resourcing

Dumbarton Enterprise Trust (DET) became effectively operational in early 1986. The organization comprised one full-time Director with secretarial support. By 1988 this had expanded to six full-time staff plus secondments. In the initial stage, support from other agencies, such as the local authorities, Scottish Development Agency and the business community, assumed critical importance, since the agency had an extremely limited capacity itself to impact upon the problems of the local economy and would have remained a highly marginal institution without such support.

Initial resourcing of the DET came from both the public and private sectors. Together, the SDA, Strathclyde Region and Dumbarton District provided 45 per cent of the budget, while fourteen companies contributed the rest in donations ranging from £300 to £3,000. Some companies donated resources in kind. The number of companies committing resources to the Trust represented a strength in that it showed the coming together of the local private sector, but it highlighted a potential weakness in that these companies lacked the resources of big corporations like BP, Metal Box, or Pilkington, which may cause problems in the longer term.

Relationships

Dumbarton was selected as a location by the CBI Special Programmes Unit because of personal contacts between the unit's director and Strathclyde Region's Chief Executive. Links had been established between the two organizations in 1983 to promote the YTS among local employers.

From the Regional Council's perspective, the Dumbarton CAP was an opportunity to do something for an area which had been designated an economic priority area but had not received any special initiative up until then. This need was more urgent given the attention being received by neighbouring Clydebank, which was the site of an Enterprise Zone and a special SDA task force (Moore and Booth, 1986b).

The Region thus steered the CAP to Dumbarton and provided support for the study. Similarly, for the SDA the Dumbarton initiative fitted in with the growing emphasis within its spatial strategy on 'self-help' projects led by the private sector (Moore and Booth, 1986a). The SDA was a founder member of BIC's parallel organization in Scotland, ScotBIC, and had supported several local enterprise agencies. Increasingly it was using the more established trusts like the Ardrossan, Saltcoats and Stevenston Trust (ASSET) as managing agents for some of its own programmes of support for small firms. For the SDA these initiatives satisfied its preference and aims to stimulate private-sector involvement and eased its own operational burdens, enabling it to target resources more effectively.

The district council had a history of involvement in local economic development, mainly in the traditional areas of factory provision. In addition, it had co-sponsored Strathclyde Community Business, an agency set up in 1984 to promote and support the community business concept throughout the region. The council also ran a significant YTS and CP programme under a Special Unit which provided some 350 training and employment places.

In recent years the political scene in Dumbarton has been marked by a fair degree of instability, with minority administrations and resignations within the majority Labour group. The Labour Party regained control of the council in 1984. During these elections the proposed Ministry of Defence expansion of the Clyde Submarine Base to accommodate Trident became a major issue. The local Labour Party took a hostile stance against these proposals and, as a result, gained an image among some sections of the local community as a militant left-wing authority. This opposition was seen as having some negative impacts on local economic development, since the two local bases at Faslane and Coulport directly or indirectly employed over 7,000 people. Indeed, the CAP study estimated that 19,000 people derived their livelihood from the bases. MoD forecasts indicated that expansion would generate 1,500 construction jobs and a long-term increase of about 500 permanent staff.

This was a complicating issue in the relationship between the authority and the private sector, in terms of both employment opportunities and image. At the time time, the experience of industrialists involved in the CAP study was that councillors and officers were supportive of a local initiative. It was relations at the corporate level which were ambiguous. The CAP provided an opportunity for developing more sustained working relationships between the authority and the private sector.

Summary

Given the recent origins of the Dumbarton initiative, it is too early to make any firm comments about how it fits into the local policy network or about its likely impact on local economic development. So far the most significant aspect has been the movement from local fragmentation, both within and between private and public sectors, to a more concerted response and relationships. The CAP study noted the absence of a community spirit or identity among the private sector, reflecting the fragmentation of a small business economy. There was no institutional mechanism for bringing business together. The CAP provided a basis for concerted action and public–private partnership. Whether this can be sustained over the longer term, given the obvious resource constraints operating on the local private sector, remains to be seen. Certainly, if DET is to make any impact on the problems of the district it will need to tap into an extensive network of resources in both the public and private sectors. In a sense the intervention of the CAP and creation of the agency may be seen as a reflection of institutional failure in both sectors to respond to the problems of the area. External intervention provided the catalyst for change, but it cannot sustain the impetus in the long term, which must come from within the local community.

Newcastle: partners in search of partnership

Local economic development initiatives in the North-East conurbation centred on Newcastle are characterized by the scale of the public sector's involvement and the fragmentation of local responses in terms of public-private partnership. This is partly the consequence of scale. In contrast to Neath, St Helens and Dumbarton, the Tyneside conurbation is a much larger regional unit with unclear geographical boundaries and several competing centres of economic and political activity, although it forms one major labour market. The Tyneside CAP was a regional rather than a purely local study, backed by the major employers in the area, including Tyne Tees Television, Northern Engineering Industries, Vickers and Procter & Gamble, as well as local authorities and public agencies like the Northumbrian Water Authority. Because of this wider spatial focus and the existence of a number of active initiatives, policy response has tended to be localized and fragmented. The main instrument of cohesion was Tyne and Wear County Council, which brought together representatives of the public and private sectors in its Standing Conference on Economic Regeneration and sponsored major county-wide initiatives, in particular the Tyne and Wear Enterprise Trust (ENTRUST).

With the abolition of English metropolitan county councils in 1986, this left major doubts about not only the long-term life of individual initiatives but the focus for any future strategic overview and mechanism for institutional integration. An interesting response to this gap was the creation of the Northern Development Company (NDC), which grew out of the death-throes of the county council with critical backing from the regional CBI and TUC (Moore and Booth, 1987 and 1989). The NDC is a throwback to the tripartism of the early 1970s, being a product of an agreement between representatives of regional capital, labour and the local state. It reflects regional dissatisfaction with the centre and fears of being left behind in the competition for economic development by Scotland. Regional interests in the North-East looked to the SDA, with its budget of over 100 million and image of success in capturing major inward investment in growth sectors like electronics. The NDC is an ersatz SDA, lacking its resources and responsibilities. It is the product of a regional consensus, not an instrument of central government intervention. How far it develops will depend not only on maintaining consensus at the regional level, but on attracting significant resources from the centre.

Whatever its initial limitations, the NDC marked a new stage in public–private partnership in the North-East, shifting the emphasis from *ad hoc* projects towards a potentially more strategic regional response. It is regarded as acting more as an enabling agency with a wider focus rather than as a development agency on the SDA model.

Project partnership: the network of responses

One of the striking features of responses to local unemployment in the North-East particularly, in comparison to Neath, Dumbarton and St Helens, was the high profile of the local authorities in economic development issues. In particular, both Newcastle City Council and Tyne and Wear County Councils had explicit plans and programmes of activity. There was no policy vacuum such as occurred in the other locations. Both local authorities had a commitment to support the local economy and felt that they had a role to play directly, as well as through arm's-length organizations. The objective of both authorities was to help local businesses to grow through a series of support programmes directed mainly at the enterprise level. Relationships with the private sector assumed a traditional client-based role whereby the authorities saw themselves as providing specific services and assistance – for example, in infrastructure, premises, investment and business advice. The notion of a systematic partnership with the private sector in formulating and implementing policy was relatively undeveloped despite the fact that there was a high level of concentration in the local economy.

The Tyneside CAP represented an attempt by the regional private sector to fashion a more concerted commitment to supporting local economic initiatives and to demonstrate to the public sector that it did have a positive role to play in sponsoring projects. Business in the Community established a small regional office based in Newcastle in 1983 to co-ordinate private-sector involvement and act as a point of information for companies. The policy space open to the private sector has undoubtedly increased in recent years due to a combination of financial constraints in the public sector and political action by central government in abolishing the metropolitan counties. Several local authorities, including Newcastle, have been rate-capped, so the capacity of districts to fill the gap left by Tyne and Wear is limited.

The relative absence of policy partnership before 1986 does not reflect ideological or political opposition on the part of local authorities. The North-East is a solid Labour area with a highly traditionalist pragmatic political leadership comparable to South Wales. There have been no parallel initiatives to the 'radical' economic policies of other Labour authorities like the old GLC, or West Midlands County Council, or Sheffield. There was a feeling, however, that the local authorities could directly provide economic development programmes. In the past, the local authorities have been able to fund these initiatives on the basis of high rates and Urban Progamme funding. This is less likely to provide a source in the future.

Below the policy level there were several project initiatives in the region which illustrated different facets of partnership. The most significant of these was ENTRUST, sponsored by the county council and the European Social Fund as part of a series of pilot initiatives in selected locations to support new small businesses. One of the most striking things about ENTRUST was the degree to which it depended on public-sector finance and yet was managed by private-sector secondees. From January 1982 until 1985 ENTRUST received nearly £1.4 million from public sources. The abolition of its principal local sponsor left ENTRUST facing an uncertain future in 1986, looking to increased contributions from the district authorities and the private sector. The problem in the public sector was getting consensus among the different district authorities to support an initiative which had a region-wide remit. ENTRUST had established a network of local offices to act as a front line for enquiries, but several districts had mounted their own initiatives which had prior claims on their resources. Within the private sector the main contribution to ENTRUST had been in the form of seconded staff. Whether local companies could be persuaded to release further resources to make up for the loss of the county council was problematical. Since 1986 the contribution to ENTRUST from the public sector has declined to 40 per cent of the budget. Section 48 of the Local Government Act abolishing the metropolitan county councils allowed the five district councils in Tyne and Wear to fund ENTRUST for two years. But this source of funding has stopped since 1988. This means ENTRUST must secure more project-based funding. In 1988 it had some fourteen projects providing income.

The balance between operational freedom and accountability in the relationship between ENTRUST and the county council was delicate. The agency had its own legal and corporate identity but no independent control over its budget. Provided it kept within its financial allocations, however, it was left fairly free to run itself. At the same time, the council saw ENTRUST almost as an extension of its economic development function. The advantage to the authority in supporting an arm's-length body was that it was able to tap private-sector resources, especially staff, without the problems of direct recruitment and internal reorganization. The council continued to provide its own range of services and to maintain control over key dimensions of policy, including financial support for businesses.

While ENTRUST was the peak example of partnership in the region, there were other projects worthy of note, particularly in terms of contrasts. For example, in South Tyneside district the local council, in association with the area's biggest private-sector employer, Northern Engineering Industries (NEI), set up the Tyneside Economic Development Company (TEDCO) in 1982. NEI's motivation for involvement was partly a response to pressure from the local authority following major reductions in the company's workforce. In addition, the agency received help from Plessey, which released a disused factory for conversion into enterprise workshops, and the local trades council. A number of other companies provided financial donations ranging from £5 to £2,500. While in terms of the total resources available to it TEDCO did not compare with ENTRUST, its resource base was much wider. To bring together various public organizations with a stake in the area's economic development an Industry Strategy Committee was set up involving the district and county councils, regional offices of central government departments, MSC, English Industrial Estates and ENTRUST. An officer–level committee was also set up to co-ordinate operational programmes.

A radically different type of initiative was Project North-East (PNE), established in 1980 by two ex-graduates with the objective of promoting new ideas for enterprise and job creation. PNE was set up as a non-profit-making company limited by guarantee with enterprise trust status. However, the focus of its activities was not direct business advice or counselling, but project development. PNE instigated several initiatives in the region, including self-employment promotions campaigns, the Newcastle Youth Enterprise Centre and a local information technology centre. While PNE received some core funding to support its limited staff, it survived primarily by piecing together support on a project basis. It acted more as a catalyst and promoter of ideas than as a direct manager. This made it a very distinctive operation.

One more example will suffice to illustrate the diverse nature of the initiatives in the area. The Derwentside Industrial Development Agency (DIDA), based in Consett, originated in the closure of the Consett Steel Works in 1980. British Steel's job-creation arm, BSC (Industry), converted the old steel plant into an enterprise workshop following the model of other redundant sites in Glasgow and South Wales. Business advice and access to subsidized loans were other elements of the BSC(I) package, designed to encourage redundant steel workers to start up in business. In line with BSC(I) policy, the agency looked to other local bodies in the public and private sectors to become involved. First, a task force was established including the DTI, local authorities and English Industrial Estates. Secondly, in November 1982 DIDA was created, taking over from BSC(I). DIDA was sponsored by BSC(I), which provided an initial start-up grant of £100,000, the district council, which provided £15,000 through Urban Aid, the National Coal Board and several private companies, giving it a total operational budget of £135,000.

Summary

This brief picture of what is happening in the North-East region around Newcastle illustrates a number of important lessons about local economic development and public–private partnership. First, it shows the diversity of initiatives under the umbrella term 'enterprise trust'. Clearly, ENTRUST is very different in organization, objectives and resources from PNE. 'Enterprise trust' may be a convenient generic label, but it can confuse more than enlighten. From the perspective of public–private partnership, the relationships apparent in an organization like ENTRUST, which was heavily dependent on public-sector funding, are different from those in TEDCO or PNE, which had a more balanced relationship in terms of resourcing.

Secondly, the local authorities played a much more directly active role in economic development. There was therefore not the same degree of space within the policy community for external initiative and private-sector leadership as was apparent in Neath, Dumbarton and St Helens. Relations between the public and private sectors were of a more traditional clientelistic model in terms of economic development, with the local authorities offering a range of services and programmes designed to support business expansion and creation. Partnership was more fragmented and project based. However, we can observe shifts in this relationship due to constraints on the public sector's capacity to engage in major programmes in this area because of rate-capping controls and the abolition of one of the most significant actors in the policy community. The search by partners for a more coherent strategic approach to the economic problems of the region led to the creation of the NDC, which may as yet be an organization in search of a clear role and substantive resources, but which provides the potential institutional platform for greater co-ordination.

There was thus a complex organizational pattern in the region without any clear formalized institutional linkage between individual projects. NDC may provide the public- and private-sector partners with a more formalized sense of partnership.

Conclusion: political space, stability and the search for public–private synergy

The impetus and development of local partnership are influenced by a number of factors. In the political environment the importance of space and stability has been highlighted. By space we mean the opportunities open within the local policy community for private-sector involvement. This will depend on the organization and commitment of the private sector and on the ideological stance and resource commitment of local government. Some local authorities have taken a markedly interventionist stance in the local economy, seeking, through mechanisms like enterprise boards (a local National Enterprise Board) or support for co-operative enterprise, to enhance local collective control over decision-making (Boddy and Fudge, 1984). These initiatives, while significant in themselves, remain relatively marginal in terms of the overall pattern of local authority involvement in economic development. However, even in the majority of authorities, there is some commitment to intervention, and this has an influence on the type of partnership with the private sector which emerges. As we saw in Newcastle, where the local authorities had a high profile in economic development, there was less private-sector leadership, whereas in Neath and Dumbarton the limited involvement of these councils left a policy space for private-sector initiative.

The notion of political stability was also important in cementing relationships between local authorities and the business community. This stability did not necessarily mean ideological convergence between the partners, but the belief that each side could, in Mrs Thatcher's noted phrase about Mr Gorbachev, 'do business with each other'. Solid Labour Party strongholds like South Wales, dominated by a traditionalist pragmatic political value system, provided a stable environment for the private sector to engage in dialogue with the local authority in Neath and to strike agreements. Where the political environment was less stable, either because no one party had overall control of the local authority (Dumbarton), or because of shifts in the internal politics of the dominant party (St Helens), this had some impact on public–private dialogue. At its most extreme, perceptions of local political instability have led central government to bypass local authorities and impose public–private partnership from outside, presenting a somewhat paradoxical picture of community initiative. Liverpool would be the most obvious case of this, where central government has established an Urban Development Corporation, a 'Minister of Merseyside' and an Inner-City Task Force over recent years, to overcome what it has seen as the 'immobilism' of local politics exerting a 'dead hand on innovation' (Parkinson and Duffy, 1984). Liverpool in fact exhibited both dimensions of political instability, with minority administrations and important shifts within the political leadership of the local Labour Party (Parkinson, 1985).

From the private-sector perspective the organization of the local business community is clearly an important factor in its capacity to assume initiative and leadership in partnership responses. We have observed the vital catalytic role of 'business outside the community' in generating 'business in the community'. The CBI Special Programmes Unit and Business in the Community, led by major corporations, have been vital sparks in encouraging local activity. Only in St Helens, which can be viewed as a very special case because of the place of Pilkington, can we argue that partnership was the product of indigenous forces, although even here the specific formation of the Trust was due to a more complex combination of organizational actors and individuals. In the other locations it was a mix of external corporate initiative, through the SPU and local branch plants, and community interests. In Dumbarton the fragmentation of the local business community meant that any initiative had to originate from outside and generate a local commitment. We can thus view three broad models of business entry into the community to form partnership initiatives. The first is the *company town* model, represented by Pilkington in St Helens, where a company dominates the local economy so that it assumes, through a combination of its own sense of corporate responsibility and political pressure, a leadership role, at least in the initial stages. The second we call the *external catalyst* model, represented by Dumbarton, where the local private sector is too weak to mount an initiative and there is a need for an external force to bring business together. Thirdly, there is a *mixed* model, which we saw in Neath, where there is a combination of external corporate involvement allied to internal political actors or brokers able to generate networks and linkages between the public and private sectors. The organization of the private sector is clearly a reflection of the structure of the local economy. St Helens was a one-industry-company town; Neath and Newcastle were largely branch plant economies; and Dumbarton was a small-business economy.

So, while partnership occurred in a common environment of economic decline and transition, the different characteristics of the local political economy were significant influences on the genesis and development of particular forms of partnership.

The concept of partnership in the local economy must be viewed as both a *structure* and a *process*. There is the dimension of formal institutions created out of the coming together of the public and private sectors in order to carry out agreed projects. NDP, St Helens Trust, ENTRUST and DET are expressions of this formal institutional dynamic. But just as critical, in contributing to achievements, is partnership as a *process* or an evolving relationship involving both formal and informal linkages, contacts and networks. As a result, a mutual interdependence is created. Local authorities regard these new agencies and relationships as a way into economic development which avoids major internal reorganization and resource commitments. It is an 'externalization' of responsibility (Moore and Booth, 1986c). For the private sector, partnership means an assumption of new roles within the policy community, which it may become increasingly difficult to disengage from, not only because of pressures at the local level, but also because of the commitment of central government to enhancing business influence and involvement in new areas of public policy. An example of this in another policy area is the recent moves to establish City Technology Colleges in inner urban locations, to be funded by central government and private business *Guardian*, 1987). The degree of commitment from the private sector is thus under pressure to increase. This can also be seen in the development of enterprise trusts from limited business advice services into more strategic agencies of local economic development. This appeared to be the direction in which NDP was developing.

The evidence of pressure on the private sector to become even more involved should not lead us to accept uncritically the notion of privatization. Enterprise trusts and partnerships are about bringing together public and private resources and assuming joint responsibility for policy formulation and project implementation, not simply about shifting responsibility from the public to the private sector. We have demonstrated that in the resourcing of initiatives the public sector plays a critical role which is perhaps obscured by the private-sector involvement in, and management of, the new institutions of partnership. Jordan and Reilly (1982), in analyzing the ideology and practice of Enterprise Zones, described the underlying paradox in terms of 'non-intervention as intervention'. We can paraphrase this by calling enterprise agencies the paradox of 'privatization as non-privatization'. It is a paradox of interdependence which a government ostensibly committed to the ideology of the market might find difficult to accept, but it seems to be the basis of the new partnership movement in the local economy.

References

Abraham, N. (1974), *Big Business and Government: The New Disorder* (London: Macmillan).

Barker, A. (ed.) (1982), *Quangos in Britain: Government and the Networks of Public Policy Making* (London: Macmillan).

Boddy, M., and Fudge, C. (eds) (1984), *Local Socialism? Labour Councils and New Left Alternatives* (London: Macmillan).

Boyle, R. (1985), 'Symposium: "Leveraging" urban development – a comparison of urban policy directions in the United States and Britain', *Policy and Politics*, vol. 13, no. 1, April, pp. 175–210.

Boyle, R., and Rich, D. (1984), 'Urban policy and the new privatization in the United States and Britain', *Public Administration Bulletin*, no. 45, August, pp. 22–36.

Business in the Community (1987), 'BP oils wheels in Wales', *BIC Post*, March–April (London: BIC).

Cawson, A. (1985), 'Corporatism and local politics in W. Grant (ed.), *The Political Economy of Corporatism* (London: Macmillan), pp. 126–47.

Centre for Employment Initiatives (1982), *Local Employment Initiatives: Report on a Series of Local Consultations held in European Countries 1982–83*, Directorate-General for Employment, Social Affairs and Education, Programme of Research and Action on the Development of the Labour Market, Study No. 82/7 (Brussels: CEI for the Commission of the European Communities).

Chandler, J., and Lawless, P. (1985), *Local Authorities and the Creation of Employment* (Aldershot: Gower).

Dichlin, M. (1983), *Social Attitudes of the Largest UK Companies* (London: CBI Special Programmes Unit/BP).

Dumbarton Community Action Programme (1985) 'Dumbarton Study', unpublished report prepared by the Dumbarton CAP Employers' Steering Group.

Fazey, I. H. (1987), *The Pathfinders* (London: Financial Training Publications).

Grant, W. (1981), *The Development of the Government Relations Function in UK Firms: A Pilot Study of UK-Based Companies*, Labour Market Policy Discussion Paper IIM/LMP 81–20 (Berlin: International Institute of Management).

Grant, W. (with J. Sargent) (1987), *Business and Politics in Britain* (Basingstoke: Macmillan Education).

Guardian (1987), 'Businessmen cool towards city tech plan', 27 January.

Hague, D. C., McKenzie, W. J. M., and Barker, A. (eds) (1975), *Public Policy and Private Interests: The Institutions of Compromise* (London: Macmillan).

International Thomson Organization (1983), *The Neath Town Study Supplementary Report: A Plan for Industrial Development Marketing Study* (Neath: ITO/Neath Development Partnership).

Jordan, G., and Reilly, G. (1982), 'Enterprise Zones: non-intervention as a form of intervention – the Clydebank Enterprise Zone and policy substitution', in *Scottish Government Yearbook 1982* (Edinburgh: Paul Harris Publishing), pp. 123–48.

Moore, C., and Booth, S. (1986a), 'Urban policy contradictions: the market versus redistributive approaches', *Policy and Politics*, vol. 14, no. 3, July, pp. 361–87.

Moore, C., and Booth, S. (1986b), 'From comprehensive regeneration to privatization: the search for effective area strategies', in W. Lever and C. Moore (eds), *The City in Transition: Policies and Agencies for the Economic Regeneration of Clydeside* (Oxford: Oxford University Press), pp. 76–91.

Moore, C., and Booth, S. (1986c), 'The pragmatic approach: local political models of regeneration', in W. Lever and C. Moore (eds), *The City in Transition: Policies and Agencies for the Economic Regeneration of Clydeside* (Oxford: Oxford University Press). pp. 92–106.

Moore, C., and Booth, S. (1987), 'Regional economic development in the North East: critical lessons from Scotland', *Northern Economic Review*, winter, pp. 2–11.

Moore, C. and Booth, S. (1989), *Managing Competition: Corporatism, Pluralism and the Negotiated Order in Scotland* (Oxford: Oxford University Press).

Moore, C., Richardson, J., and Moon, J. (1985), 'Politicization of business: corporate responses to unemployment', paper presented to the Politics and Business in Western Democracies Workshop, European Consortium for Political Research, Barcelona, March.

Parkinson, M. (1985), *Liverpool on the Brink* (Hermitage, Berks.: Policy Journals).

Parkinson, M., and Duffy, J. (1984), 'Government's reponses to inner city riots: the Minister for Merseyside and the task force', *Parliamentary Affairs*, no. 1, pp. 76–96.

Richardson, J. (1983), *The Development of Corporate Responsibility in the UK*, Strathclyde Papers on Government and Politics No. 1 (Glasgow: Department of Politics, University of Strathclyde).

Thomas, R. (1977), *The Government of Business* (Deddington, Oxford: Philip Allan).

Todd, G. (1984), *Creating New Jobs in Europe: How Local Initiatives Work*, Special Report No. 165 (London: Economist Intelligence Unit).

Vogel, D., and Bradshaw, T. (1980), *Corporations and their Critics* (New York: McGraw-Hill).

Young, K., and Mills, L. (1983), *Managing the Post-Industrial City* (London: Heinemann Educational).

Welsh Committee (1986), *Enterprise Agencies and Job Creation*, minutes of evidence, 2 July 1986, House of Commons Paper 502, Session 1985–6 (London: HMSO).

4 Policy responses

Introduction: the policy unity behind organizational diversity

Despite the diversity of organizational forms of public–private partnership there is a strong common theme underlying the policy objectives and strategies of enterprise agencies. The fundamental principles of local response are:

(1) the validity of localized initiative;
(2) the spatial causation of and partial solution to the problems identified;
(3) the need to generate an 'enterprise culture' through small business growth and development as the key to the future economic health of the local community.

In terms of implementation, this means, first, programmes which provide support for small enterprise development, including both physical infrastructure (premises, workshops) and software services (business counselling and advice, finance). Secondly, it means sectoral diversification of the local economy in order to reduce historical dependencies on traditional heavy manufacturing and to break out of the branch plant syndrome. So, for example, the development of new service industries, high-technology enterprise and activities like tourism have been programmatic features of the partnerships which we studied. Thirdly, it involves an area or spatial approach which attempts to provide an integrated focus for development, for example, inner urban renewal projects. Finally, there is the provision of training and job-creation schemes to enhance the competitive capacity of individuals within local labour markets. This typically utilizes existing central government schemes like the YTS and Community Programme, generating locally managed projects which may fit into other elements of a local economic development strategy.

This chapter will seek to provide a more detailed account of the operational processes and activities of local partnerships, using data from our case studies. We will review the ways in which local agencies interact with other bodies to promote economic development through various programmes. We will also argue that partnerships are an intensely political process at different levels: first, at the level of local inter-organizational networks of bargaining and negotiation; and secondly, at the level of ideology concerning the values and conceptions of local economic regeneration. Chapter 5 will analyse the economic impacts of partnership, raising questions about the effectiveness of these responses to local regeneration.

Initiatives: strategic choice and pragmatic responses

The programmes put forward by local partnerships face a dilemma between the room for strategic choice and the need for a pragmatic response to immediate problems. Nowhere is this dilemma better illustrated than in the programmes of assistance to businesses which provide the central focus of much local activity by enterprise agencies.

The small business explosion

There are two basic elements in the local partnership strategy for enterprise development. First, there is the provision of an appropriate physical infrastructure of 'hardware' in the form of sites and premises. The second is a series of 'software' support programmes including counselling, advice and access to funding.

In terms of physical infrastructure, local enterprise agencies are mainly concerned with identifying needs, making providers (especially local authorities) aware of the gaps in local provision and helping client firms find appropriate accommodation for their businesses. Essentially, local enterprise agencies act as a catalyst for others to provide facilities. This was the role identified by the St Helens Trust, which managed to persuade both the local council and Pilkington that there was a need for small factory units in the locality.

It is perhaps less usual for an enterprise agency to act as a project manager, but this was the original role performed by Neath Development Partnership. A disused factory space, comprising some

36,000 square feet, was converted into small enterprise workshops, with the Partnership assuming initial responsibilities for project development, management and promotion, although the bulk of the funding came from public sources (see Table 3.1). After a period of time, management became the direct responsibility of the local authority.

These facilities were designed to encourage new small firms through low rental and access to business advice. They were seen as meeting a gap in the property market which private-sector developers were unwilling to meet because of the lack of profit, costs of provision and maintenance, and risks involved in such investments. The Neath Partnership was functioning as an extension of the local authority estates department, but bringing in additional expertise in areas such as business advice and marketing and enjoying a degree of operational flexibility and independent image which would attract potential clients. This did not mean that the local authority was not involved in managing the development. An Estate Management Committee was established to oversee the scheme, comprising four council officers and one councillor out of a membership of seven. Legal ownership of the site remained with the local authority. From 1985 a seconded council officer was appointed as the workshop manager. Larger industrial estates and land lay outside the control of the borough council or Partnership. Ownership of the msot significant industrial land lay with the Welsh Development Agency and West Glamorgan County Council, and here the role of the partnership was to try to persuade these bodies to develop sites.

Software support includes counselling, advice and access to funding. All local enterprise agencies provide at least basic business advice and some level of counselling, either directly – often employing full- or part-time secondees from their private-sector sponsors – or indirectly, by acting as an initial contact point and feeding inquiries on to other agencies. The extent of the service offered by individual agencies will depend largely on the resources available to them, particularly staff with appropriate expertise. There is tremendous variation in the capacity of agencies in this respect. At one end of the scale are agencies, such as the Dumbarton Enterprise Trust, which are essentially a filtering mechanism for other bodies. At the other end of the scale are agencies, such as Neath, which can provide fairly sophisticated levels of in-house counselling using their own staff and secondees.

Access to finance is a less developed function of enterprise agencies. One of the most prominent examples of an agency which enjoys such access to loan and equity capital is the St Helens Trust, through a local Business Expansion Scheme syndicate. This was originally launched in 1984, raising £200,000 from a consortium of local investors. Its aim was to provide finance in the range of £25,000 to £60,000 for individual businesses in the locality. While the Trust did not directly manage the scheme, it provided a link between client firms and the fund's management board. Trust staff assessed the business viability and financial needs of proposals and helped clients to prepare their cases.

Neath Development Partnership also had access to a small loans fund. The Partnership acted as local agent for British Steel (Industry), the job-creation offshoot of BSC, and for British Petroleum in assessing clients for loan funding.

'Advice and counselling' is an ambiguous term since it can embrace a wide variety of activities involving very different levels of commitment by agencies. It may involve informal and relatively short advisory sessions for individuals seeking to start up in business, or substantial investment of time in supporting established firms. Perhaps one of the most extensive counselling and support services was offered by ENTRUST. The significance of its services was the focus on established businesses and job protection, and the development of new products. A 'piloting service' was available, whereby ENTRUST secured managerial secondments to help develop projects with individual client companies. This approach was different from the typical 'company midwife' role of enterprise agencies, assisting in the birth of new firms. The piloting scheme was more like a 'company consultant' approach, going into established firms with identified needs and helping to resolve these. It is perhaps much easier to engage in the midwife role than in the consultant role because the involvement is often much less intensive. This is just one of the many dilemmas of the small firms approach.

First, it is based on indigenous growth. This is understandable in that one of the critical problems of many local economies is their historical dependence on branch plant enterprises. The vulnerability of these plants to corporate decisions made elsewhere was marked in the case of Neath (BP and Metal Box). St Helens shows the problems of depending heavily on one industry and one dominant company which, while having its headquarters in the town, was in effect a global operation. At the same time, the generation of indigenous enterprise may, depending on the ultimate market for the product or service, simply result in recycling existing wealth within the community rather than creating new wealth through the attraction of inward investment. Given the limited amount of significant mobile investment, and the resultant intensity of competition between communities for what there is, it makes strategic sense for enterprise agencies to focus their limited resources on sectors of business amenable to their influence. What perhaps needs further examination is to what extent enterprise is catering for purely local markets or 'exporting' its services and products.

The emphasis on small firms is marked. It is encouraged by central government and by local authorities, which see the small firms sector as one of the few areas of jobs growth. There has been intense debate about the contribution of small firms to national economic growth. Birch (1979), in his often quoted study of US manufacturing industry, indicated that the small firms sector was the dynamic area of new jobs growth in the economy. It can also be argued that it is inefficient and ineffective to prop up dying industries or companies when what is needed is to encourage dynamic new growth. Other researchers have been critical of this type of study. For example, Storey has written extensively on the impact of new enterprise on local economies, based on empirical research in the North-East of England.

From this he concluded that the net employment impact of new enterprise was marginal and unlikely to provide opportunities for the most disadvantaged in the labour market (Storey, 1982). Indeed, he argues that the 'indices of entrepreneurship' are more likely to be found in regions with a buoyant economy, indicating the important linkages which exist between small firms and the wider economy. Storey thus argues for a much more highly targeted policy of support, selecting enterprises with growth potential based on a clearer understanding of how small firms operate and what their objectives are (Storey and Johnson, 1987). This points to the conflict between the 'company midwife' approach, which is more selective but demands more resources and thought to be given to how the agency can market itself to existing businesses. Even so, it is not clear on what basis selectivity should operate. Picking 'winners' in economic activity is often an elusive task. Perhaps a hard-headed critical appraisal of all business proposals, whether from new or existing firms, is the best contribution enterprise agencies can make.

Sectoral diversification – encouraging new types of economic activity

The encouragement of small firms is part of a process of sectoral diversification of local economies. Enterprise agencies have also become involved in the development of new sectors of economic activity in more explicit ways. The ways in which agencies have acted suggests an important role as policy entrepreneur. This role was particularly significant in Neath in terms of proposals for tourism linked to a wider urban area renewal initiative.

Developing tourism in Neath was seen as a key way of diversifying the local economy and building on existing attractions. However, actually realizing new development proved difficult because of the lack of a clear focus in terms of area or a particular project. In addition, it became clear that significant amounts of public investment would be required at an initial stage in order to attract private developers. Because of constraints on landownership of key sites, original plans had to be modified. In Chapter 3 we highlighted the resourcing implications of the Special Project package under which the tourism proposals were subsumed, showing the significance of public-sector input.

The actual formulation of a proposal involved bringing together several agencies. Specifically in relation to tourism, the Partnership, through one of its corporate sponsors, commissioned a study to highlight potential developments. A Tourism Development Group was formed which brought together representatives of other interested public and private-sector bodies. A further study identified a range of developments including a dry-ski slope, an aquarium, a prehistoric theme park, craft shops and walkways. Over 500 jobs were envisaged as arising directly and indirectly from these schemes, along with 300 temporary jobs in environmental improvement funded through the MSC. The Partnership appointed a full-time tourism development manager whose job was to stimulate local investment.

The Partnership's role was to act as a catalyst, stimulating ideas and promoting these to interested parties which would actually fund any developments. There were problems in evolving a strategy and assessing individual proposals. The attraction of a major flagship development which would act as a magnet focused on the ski slope. The lack of a suitable developer with adequate technical and financial resources led to the Partnership's withdrawal from this concept, although publicity had already been generated. Expectations were subsequently scaled down. In one sense the episode exposed some weaknesses in the Partnership, in particular the lack of relevant expertise (the idea was generated prior to the appointment of the tourism development manager) and the push for advance publicity in order to generate interest before any firm commitment from a developer. On the other hand, the Partnership saw itself as in the business of generating ideas, some of which might be too ambitious and fail. The tourism development manager focused on local community-based projects which would gradually build up facilities in an economic sector which was viewed as an additional opportunity rather than as an alternative to other jobs.

In Dumbarton tourism was also identified as a major sector of the local economy. As in Neath, a local tourist group, backed by the area's Tourist Board and individual operators, was established in order to review needs and identify opportunities for specific projects – for example, self-catering sites, activity holidays and heritage projects. The most significant project proposal, however, involved external agencies such as the Scottish Development Agency, the Scottish Tourist Board and commercial interests, since the costs of any big project required considerable new investment.

In August 1985 a study of Balloch, at the southern edge of Loch Lomond, proposed the development of a major leisure complex involving up to £24 million in investment and commitments from public agencies to clear sites and provide infrastructure. The private sector was expected to provide £18 million of this investment in such ventures as a hotel and accommodation, a supermarket, private housing and leisure and sports complex. Clearly the role of a local enterprise trust, particularly of the small scale of the Dumbarton Enterprise Trust, in this type of development is likely to be marginal. In Neath, the Neath Development Partnership played a more central role, but the scale of proposed projects again meant relying on significant outside investment from public and private sectors.

Urban renewal: private planning and public policy

The development of tourism leads us on to consider the spatial focus of enterprise agencies. Clearly, at a most generalized level agencies are concerned with the regeneration of a defined local economy or community. But this concern can take more specific forms with the packaging of area renewal initiatives. Neath illustrates the ways in which agencies can get involved in a process which was regarded largely as the responsibility of the public sector until the 1980s.

The concept of the Special Project was originally developed by the WDA, which launched a pilot scheme in 1983 inviting bids for special funding for projects which would attract major private investment. A package was put together by NDP combining town-centre redevelopment with a programme of tourism development. The first element was based on outline development plans drawn up by the local authority. It comprised a mixed retail, office, housing and leisure development. The second element was based on the tourism strategy which had been developing within NDP and its discussions with other interests.

The proposal was aimed at linking two distinctive elements within an integrated development plan for the town centre and surrounding area. It was an ambitious plan with an estimated total cost of £20 million. The proposal argued strongly in favour of public-sector investment, particularly on the tourism package, in order to generate major new private investment. The formulation of the proposals was structured thorugh a committee of senior officers from NDP, Neath Council, the WDA and the Welsh Tourist board, to which a series of specialist working groups reported. Clearly NDP did not have the resources or powers to carry through such a development. Its role was to generate interest and provide the impetus for public and private agencies to come together. It is a powerful example of the enterprise agency as 'policy entrepreneur'. NDP saw an opportunity to integrate several individual projects and to capitalize on new sources of funding. It also demonstrated NDP's attempts at promoting a more strategic conception of local regeneration. The Partnership brought expertise and skills in the fields of marketing and packaging proposals, while the public sector set the overall policy, planning and financial framework. The realization of the package depended on many factors outside the influence of the Partnership. In particular, the whole basis of the proposal was underpinned by assumptions of public funding from various agencies. These assumptions proved increasingly difficult to sustain because of the constraints operating on public budgets. This highlights the problem of trying to develop strategic choice where ultimate decision-making and resource-allocation powers lie with numerous organizations. In the end, a more pragmatic response through a series of individual projects was more likely to emerge. NDP did not have the powers or resources which have allowed the Scottish Development Agency to promote integrated area projects with local authorities (Moore and Booth, 1986a).

The Special Project bid was a piece of opportunism linking established or planned urban renewal proposals with the tourism package being promoted by the Partnership. It was an attempt to tap into new sources of funding being provided by the WDA. The proposals were promoted as a comprehensive integrated programme for the renewal of the Neath area based on public–private funding. The fashionable concept of 'leverage' (Boyle, 1985) was built into the package whereby a limited amount of public-sector input was supposed to generate an even greater investment from the private sector. The constraints on available funding limited what was likely to happen on the ground, but what was important for the Partnership was not necessarily that the total package would be supported, but that an environment conducive to new investment would be stimulated. The Partnership was thus in this sense as much about the generation of ideas as about concrete developments.

Both the Special Project concept and the tourism strategy illustrate the notion of partnership as a process of negotiation, bargaining and building up formal and informal linkages. The idea of policy entrepreneurship captures the essence of seizing opportunities, promoting concepts and selling them to others. The Neath Partnership was not a director or controlling body in these areas.

Training: the entrepreneur and the unemployed

Finally, in considering the elements of programmes for local economic development, there is training. There are two main aspects: first, training for enterprise (that is, the provision of programmes for business entrepreneurs); and secondly, training and associated job-creation schemes for the unemployed. Many enterprise agencies provide training programmes at different levels for those starting up or developing in business. Others act as a filter, assessing training needs and individual capacity before passing people on to relevant agencies. ENTRUST ran a series of courses through its training unit, ranging from short presentations on self-employment to the development and implementation of major programmes. These courses were run in conjunction with the MSC and local colleges. In 1985 nearly nine hundred people went on courses organized by ENTRUST and substantially funded from the European Social Fund.

PNE was also involved in training initiatives through the Newcastle Youth Enterprise Centre. This initiative combined start-up premises for young people with on-site advice and counselling, start-up capital and training.

In the above examples training was directly related to business development and thus to job creation or maintenance. Enterprise agencies are also involved in youth training and temporary job-creation schemes through links with MSC programmes. One of the motivations behind the initial CBI promotion of corporate responsibility was to increase company participation in YTS. It also subsequently became involved through a special task force in making recommendations to the MSC on increasing company involvement under the Community Programme.

Enterprise agencies provide a mechanism for promoting, administering and overseeing YTS and CP schemes. They can act as managing agents covering several projects and sponsors which otherwise would not have the administrative and managerial resources to participate. This is particularly true of small firms providing YTS places.

The St Helens Trust was instrumental in helping an independent training scheme, INDEX, become operational (Fazey, 1987). This provided structured training and work experience for school-leavers over two years, including direct experience with local companies, especially small firms. INDEX was partly funded by the MSC and partly by contributions from local firms and the European Social Fund. The scheme provided for an annual intake of 120 school-leavers.

NDP was extensively involved in both YTS and CP schemes as a managing agency. Under YTS it provided up to one hundred trainees with placements in local companies, ensuring that both on- and off-the-job training met MSC objectives. NDP acted as a mediator between the broad training goals of the MSC and the more specific needs of individual firms providing placements. The Partnership's managing agency maintained contacts with up to one hundred local firms.

Participation in the CP was another major commitment for NDP and provided an example of how the scheme could be used to support projects which met the economic-development and job-creation objectives of the Partnership. As in YTS the Partnership acted as a managing agency, initially responsible for providing 200 to 300 places each year. This grew to 1,000 approved places. The Partnership secured a significant share of the regional allocation of CP money because of its willingness to put forward projects while other areas faced political and union opposition to participation. While several projects were of the traditional environmental clearance type there were some significant innovative projects, including the construction of a marina and a mountain centre. The projects provided not only temporary jobs but permanent facilities, longer-term employment and commercial potential in developing the tourism strategy of the Partnership.

Another area of training for the unemployed was in new technology through sponsorship of information technology centres (ITECs). In Neath the Partnership was instrumental in planning and bringing together sponsors for an ITEC which provided training for 30 to 40 young people per year. The Neath ITEC was designated the all-Wales ITEC in 1983, acting as the centre for the development of other ITECS in Wales – for example, providing advice and help in the appointment of staff. The Neath ITEC was initially managed by a secondee from Metal Box, which had provided the premises for the centre. Subsequently, the centre developed commercial activities, principally software contracts and training programmes for local firms. The ITEC was funded by the MSC, a DTI grant for capital equipment and a grant from Neath Council. It was formed into a limited company with charitable status. The board of this company included the Neath Partnership and other sponsors.

Within the Community Programme managing agency in Neath the most significant single project was the Pelenna Mountain Centre, which was seen not only as a community facility, but also as a commercial enterprise which would become part of the tourism-related strategy. The scale of this venture, and of the CP managing agency generally, did raise questions about an appropriate management structure. Initially, as in many other areas of the Partnership's activities, projects were developed around individuals. There was a high dependence on a few people who acted as catalyst and broker. Once projects became established, however, there was often a need to move towards more organized managerial control systems, calling for a different set of skills.

Overview

Partnerships as represented by the enterprise agencies examined here have become more or less established in a local policy network of public and private institutions concerned with economic development. They provide a variety of services and perform several functions within this network. Two key roles would appear to be as a *broker*, linking the public and private sectors and tapping into the resources of both, whether money or expertise, and in some cases as a *managing agency* in areas such as training. More generally we have described partnerships as policy entrepreneurs or innovators, stimulating new ideas, packaging and promoting these to other agencies. An agency such as Project North-East in Newcastle is perhaps the purest example of the policy entrepreneur role, while agencies such as the Neath Partnership have evolved into economic development companies managing a variety of activities and seeking to develop new trading enterprises. This is a more proactive approach to local economic development, although agencies still play a very reactive role in relation to small business advice and counselling, waiting for clients to approach them rather than actively seeking clients out.

Even relatively large agencies such as Neath or St Helens have limited direct resources. The first director of the St Helens Trust has described his role as a 'poor friar' (Fazey, 1987) who seeks to do good works through mobilizing the resources of other organizations.

The notion of indendence is also important to these agencies, although, as we have seen, they are also dependent on developing close relationships with other organizations if they are to achieve anything. Small-scale agencies such as Dumbarton Enterprise Trust are highly dependent on drawing on the resources of public and private organizations both to fund staff and to provide services to clients.

The brokerage role and the bringing together of public and private sectors is a critical aspect of enterprise agencies. In areas such as Dumbarton, where the private sector was fragmented, the development of a local agency acted as a catalyst for cementing relationships within the business community, as well as bringing that community into closer contact with the public sector. This illustrates the importance of altering attitudes, which works at two levels: first, in bringing different segments of the local community together; and secondly, in seeking to change attitudes within the local population about enterprise and business, particularly through encouraging self-employment and small firms. This raises important political questions both at the local level of policy networks and at a broader level of the ideology and values being promoted.

It is interesting to note that other studies have confirmed the analysis of roles and relationships described above. In particular, an important contribution to the debate about local economic regeneration, recently published, finds similar processes in West Germany. In a comparative study of four localities, Hull (Hull with Hjern, 1987) stressed the importance of intermediaries within an 'assistance structure' which could mediate between resource providers, especially public agencies, and small firms. These local intermediaries provided vital co-ordination between agencies, in effect creating a local policy network where previously there had been fragmentation and isolation. The intermediaries assisted firms by helping to define problems, identify appropriate resources and mobilize these resources. Comparisons were drawn with enterprise agencies in the UK. The study highlighted the most successful of these inter-mediaries, the County Development Agency in Borken, which was constituted as a private law agency. This status gave the agency a high degree of autonomy, which helped it handle conflicts between firms and local authorities and other tiers of government. This capacity to act as an 'honest broker' existed despite the fact that the sponsors of the agency were local authorities. In addition, the agency had no financial resources of its own to help firms. Neither did it act as a managing agency for other resource providers. Its role was limited to advice, and Hull observed that 'this very resourcelessness may be single most important explanation for its distinctive intermediary role' (Hull with Hjern, 1987, p. 170). The parallel with the 'poor friar' image observed by Fazey in his study of St Helens is striking (Fazey, 1987).

Ideology and values: the politics of partnership

The enterprise agency movement is part of a broader shift in the political environment since 1979 which emphasizes the corporate responsibility of the private sector and its role in the formulation and implementation of public policy in a wide range of areas. This represents the ideological level of the politics of partnership. Equally, enterprise agencies are part of a local political process. If an agency is to have any impact on the local economy it must become embedded in the local policy community where it will seek to influence decision-making processes. Enterprise agencies are a product of local authority and private-sector interaction addressing a public issue of critical political salience.

For central government, one of the positive benefits of enterprise agencies is the extension of the influence of the private sector in areas of policy previously seen as the preserve of public authorities.

Enterprise agencies are undoubtedly ideologically acceptable to a government wedded to the notion of the market rather than the alternative local-authority-sponsored enterprise boards which are based on notions of socialized planning and public intervention in the way firms operate. Enterprise agencies are involved in managing a process of economic transition which involves changing community cultures traditionally based on employment dependency into a vision of an 'enterprise culture' based on competing small businesses operating in the dynamics of the market-place.

There are contradictions, however, in the practice of enterprise agencies and the ideological values which government imputes to them. While the overriding emphasis is on business development through the market, we can also see varying degrees of concern with community welfare and for the most disadvantaged groups in the labour market. For example, Neath Development Partnership's extensive involvement in YTS and CP was a direct expression of concern for the unemployed. Ideas about using CP-funded projects to develop community facilities and community-based businesses reflect notions of collective self-help.

Enterprise agencies are thus involved in stimulating a new consensus within the local community about economic develop-ment. It is a consensus based in practice on a mix of market, community self-help, private participation and public intervention. In the rest of this section we analyse the politics of partnership at three levels: first, at the micro-level of the local community and the ways in which enterprise agencies fit into the local political process; secondly, at the meso- or middle level of the spatial economy (what are the assumptions being made about the problems and prospects for the local economy?); and thirdly, at the macro-level of underlying values (what are the interests of national government in promoting this localized response to economic action? Can we locate the approach being adopted through this form of intervention in some kind of framework and can this be compared to alternative models operating on different values and assumptions?).

Partnership and the local political process

All local enterprise agencies based on the notion of partnership between the public and private sectors are political animals. There is often a knee-jerk reaction to deny political involvement because politics is equated with party political labels, and enterprise agencies emphasize their independence from such ties. We would not wish to dispute the assertion of political neutrality in this narrow sense. What we mean by political is a broader definition of involvement in, and integration with, the public decision-making process leading to the distribution of public resources and outcomes designed to benefit the community. Clearly, on this definition, partnerships are intimately involved in politics.

In Chapter 3 we analysed the different local political contexts in which partnerships emerged. We argued that the two key dimensions to the evolution and development of partnership were policy space and political stability. In locations where these two conditions existed and where the private sector was sufficiently organized, as in Neath, the opportunity for a partnership agency to assume a significant role in local policy-making was significant. NDP acted as a policy entrepreneur, bargaining and negotiating with a wide variety of public and private agencies seeking to stimulate action and tap resources. This process was essential to understanding how Neath worked. In this chapter we have provided specific examples of this process.

Equally, in St Helens the economic and social importance of Pilkington had a great political significance in getting the Trust started, and the Trust acted as a means of bringing together public and private interests in the community. In Dumbarton and the North-East the scope for private-sector involvement was less clear. In the first case, this was because of political instability and the fragmentation of the local business community. In the latter, the policy space was foreclosed by the high profile of the local authorities in economic development activity. In the North-East the private sector played a more subsidiary policy role, although, with the abolition of the metropolitan county and budgetary constraints on other local authorities, the space was opening up. The emergence of the Northern Development Company as an embryonic attempt at strategic partnership indicated new possibilities (Moore and Booth, 1987 and 1989).

Despite the differences in space and stability between the four locations there was a common theme of the possibility for some form of partnership initiative. There was a broad convergence of values or consensus on the need for joint action. We observed the contrast with areas like Liverpool, which was characterized by a high degree of political instability and ideological conflict. This had led central government to impose 'partnership' from above, bypassing local government through mechanisms like the Urban Development Corporation or Inner-City Task Force (Parkinson and Duffy, 1984).

This centralized conception of partnership involves limiting the role of local authorities. It becomes embroiled in wider discussion about the relationship between central and local government. The forms of partnership we have described still have important implications for local authorities. While they do not displace their statutory responsibilities, enterprise agencies can herald significant changes in the way local authorities respond to the problem of economic development. We observed that the use of partnership agencies by authorities can be seen as a form of 'externalization' of responsibilities and resources. It acknowledges the technical, financial and political constraints on local government in responding effectively to a new issue. It also seeks to mobilize the expertise of the private sector through the joint sponsorship of arm's-length organizations. This process has occurred not only in local government. The Scottish Development Agency increasingly uses enterprise agencies (more commonly called 'trusts' in Scotland) as a means of delivering its own services and programmes. A type of 'contractual' relationship develops, with the enterprise trust accountable to the SDA for the performance of these functions (Moore and Booth, 1986a).

These arrangements stretch lines of accountability and responsibility. They can generate tensions and uncertainty. There is a delicate balance to be struck between the legitimate demands of political accountability and the need for operational independence. The relationship is often made more difficult by the informal way in which enterprise agencies function against the more bureaucratic and norms structure of local government.

We questoned whether the new relationships emerging from the partnership phenomenon could be dismissed as temporary, given the long-term nature of the problem to be 'solved'. As agencies become established as part of the local policy community – the St Helens Trust was ten years old in 1987 – there is an increasing interdependence of public and private sectors. This is not only an issue for local authorities. Can they simply withdraw their support for these initiatives? It is equally an issue for the private sector. Just how far are companies willing to go in committing time, staff and cash to such ventures? If partnerships have a long-term role there may be increasing pressures on them to be more self-financing. Neath Development Partnership was seeking to develop commercial subsidiaries and trading enterprises which would not only contribute to local economic development and provide employment opportunities, but also contribute towards supporting the agency. One adverse side-effect of creeping commercialism, however, might be to reduce support for certain clients who could not pay for agency services.

The type of relationship between public and private sectors which develops out of joint initiatives will significantly depend on the role and scope of the partnership. In Neath this was very open. NDP represented an attempt to look at the strategic development of the local economy. This brought it into many different areas of activity and contact with a variety of agencies. Other initiatives, however, were more restricted in scope.

The relationship between public and private sectors also involves both formal structures and informal personal linkages. The importance of 'policy brokers' with access to several key constituencies or interests is often critical is smoothing the bargaining process.

What partnerships bring to the local authorities is access to new expertise and resources. The price of this is some ceding of responsibility and authority and a willingness to compromise. An alternative approach for local authorities would be for them to adopt a more overtly interventionist plan for economic development through local 'planning agreements' with companies and to establish enterprise boards operating at a company or sectoral level. This kind of approach raises different problems in public–private relationships and it also demands significant political, financial and organizational commitment on the part of the authority to be successful.

It is a myth that partnership through enterprise agencies depoliticizes decisions about local economic development. It simply moves these decisions into new arenas. Agencies are active in the local policy community, not just because they are products of public- and private-sector sponsorship, but also because they engage in lobbying and bargaining with both sectors to secure resources. 'Policy entrepreneurship' is a fusion of politics (with a small 'p') and enterprise. We have emphasized that enterprise agencies are to be viewed not simply as the privatization of public policy but rather as a further intermeshing of public and private sectors. As such, the relationships which develop are inevitably messy.

The politics of community regeneration

The focus of enterprise agencies is on the local economy and on the promotion of 'enterprise'. This can be seen as a complementary strategy to wider regional policy, national economic management and public-sector intervention, or it can become a substitute for them. Analysis of urban policy in the UK over the last decade shows a marked trend towards a narrowing of focus in terms of space and programmes. There has been a clear move away from the assumption of macro-economic demand management strategies and even firm regional policy as positive tools of intervention. In their place has come local community responses to the problem of economic regeneration. The definition of what constitutes urban policy has narrowed, so that instead of the comprehensive social, economic and environmental strategy of the 1977 White Paper (Department of the Environment, 1977) we have a strategy based on economic and business development.

The question of how to tackle economic decline through spatial strategies has been on the agenda since the 1930s. What has changed is the focus of concern, away from the inter-regional dimension to the intra-regional and sub-regional. The concern with the small area approach developed partly out of dissatisfaction with existing regional policy, which had been based on attempts to influence the movement of capital to the regions of high unemployment (MacLennan and Parr, 1979). By the late 1970s the problem of spatial regeneration was being defined as a problem essentially of the inner cities. Industry and people had moved out of these areas to greenfield sites, encouraged by public policy. It became clear that those left behind were the most disadvantaged, requiring public support. Equally, there was still a basic infrastructure to maintain on an ever decreasing fiscal base. Thus, urban policy began to address the problem of economic regeneration. Progressively since 1979 this dimension has come to dominate policy initiatives, with the emphasis shifting away from public-sector leadership to public–private partnership as the instrument of regeneration (Boyle, 1985; Moore and Booth, 1986b).

The basis of the new partnership consensus is that local enterprise can be encouraged and a significant response can be made to the unemployment problem through local initiative. This does not preclude the partners from pursuing other responses, including pressing for changes in national economic policy. The local consensus essentially amounts to support for small enterprise capitalism. We have already discussed the problem of relying on small businesses as the agents of significant economic growth and employment creation. In the absence of a firm regional policy the focus of activity is on local initiatives to attract investment by bringing key actors together and developing packages. This strategy is reinforced by government-funded Urban Development Corporations in the local economies of the major conurbations.

The spatially based approach of local initiatives also assumes that problems can be significantly tackled at the community level. Clearly, many of the problems manifested at a local level are caused by, and lie beyond, the influence of the local community. The analysis of the employment impacts of the individual partnerships shows their limited effectiveness in the context of wider trends, despite the positive contributions made to new enterprise development locally (see Chapter 5). The local economy is influenced by regional and national economic policies and by the decisions of large corporations with branch plants. These policy decisions are influenced by political ideologies and structural shifts in the national and international economy. What local projects can help tackle are localized constraints on development, including physical infrastructure, business advice and training. They have limited impact on the effective level of demand in the economy.

A localized approach has certain political advantages for central government. It defines the problem and solution within narrow spatial boundaries. It plays down underlying structural issues, implying that these cannot be tackled by public intervention but are a product of 'market forces' to which local communities must learn to adjust.

There may be an economic imperative in focusing at the local level in responding to certain problems of development, but there is also a political imperative in creating visible local responses. At the same time, the problem and solution cannot ultimately be exported by central government to local communities, since local partnerships in practice depend critically on public funding and intervention, either directly or indirectly. It is therefore a delusion or confidence trick to suggest that enterprise agencies are proof that economic regeneration can be left to local private-sector initiative. Yet this is the impression one gets from a superficial reading of the model of 'success' these partnerships supposedly represent.

The competing conceptions of regeneration

By now it should be clear that we believe that there are important political as well as economic dimensions to the role of enterprise agencies and the new partnership movement. The enterprise agencies represent for central government an important instrument for delivering certain ideas about economic regeneration at the local level and for influencing the ways in which the local public sector responds to the problem of unemployment. Thus, we need to look at the underlying ideology or values of the approach. We need to understand what type of economic development is being promoted. It is one alternative based on a distinctive set of values. In practice, the ideology is contradictory and ambiguous, but there are clear assumptions which need unpacking.

How can we best characterize these assumptions? We have referred to the narrowing of policy represented by enterprise agencies. These institutional arrangements and prescriptions need to be located at a deeper level of underlying objectives. How is regeneration specified? The partnerships believe in the 'enterprise culture' based on competitive and efficient local enterprise, sectoral diversification of the local economy and the use of public funds to 'lever' substantial private investment. Through these mechanisms new employment opportunities will be created for the benefit of the local community. This approach can be described as a 'modified market' approach. It accepts the dominance of the market and private ownership and seeks to rectify specific local weaknesses and remove blockages. In contrast, there is a 'social redistributive' model which describes some of the more interventionist local authorities. This approach is based on the aim of increasing local community control over the economy through a combination of collectivization and planning. The initiatives of the old Greater London Council, through the Greater London Enterprise Board, are the best example of this approach (Moore and Booth, 1986c).

Figure 4.1 is an outline of the principal features of these two competing approaches. Local partnership superficially suggests a move away from corporatist modes of policy-making between the state (central or local), its agencies (quangos) and organized producer interests (big business and labour) to a more open pluralist model at the local level (Cawson, 1982). But what is the nature of these partnerships? The participation of major corporations through local branch plants and national umbrella groups suggests a significant element of organized external intervention. The definition of economic development and community regeneration is derived from the market.

	Market	Social resdistributive
Institutions	Central government Quangos Local partnerships	Public sector
Mode of intervention	Market based	Welfare based
Focus of policy	Enterprise Private investment	Disadvantaged Collective distribution
Benefits to the community	'Trickle-down'	Targeted
Spatial focus	Inner cities Areas of established economic activity	Peripheral communities Area of socio-economic deprivation
Mode of decision-making	Central or local 'corporatism'	'Local pluralism'
Accountability	Indirect	Direct

Fig. 4.1 The modified market versus social redistributive models.

Conclusion: partnership, politics and ideology

We have aimed in this chapter at going beyond the superficial level of institutional and organizational analysis which characterizes much of the writing on urban policy and enterprise agencies. We sought to examine the underlying interests and ideologies current in this concept of 'partnership'. The diversity of organizational forms hides an essential unity of purpose. The wide range of programmes, from business advice to urban redevelopment, is designed to restimulate the market in disadvantaged areas and to help in the process of a cultural 'mind shift' in popular attitudes towards enterprise.

Paradoxically, the pursuit of the market is extensively based on public spending and intervention through a variety of agencies. This is not necessarily a contradiction, since modern capitalism is highly dependent on state intervention at national and local levels. However, dependence on public input is not the lesson which a government committed to the notion of the market and private responsibility would wish to emphasize. The lessons of the partnership movement are at best ambiguous for those subscribing to the liberal-market version of 'enterprise culture'.

We have strongly argued that there is a political as well as an economic dimension to the management of local economic crisis and change. At one level the new partnerships are reactive in the sense of responding to immediate problems of unemployment and business decline. At another level they are strategic in aiming to ease the transition to major political, social and economic changes.

Partnerships represent a new form of interventionism in the local economy which is a challenge and an alternative to the 'free market' and 'municipal socialism' models. As such, they present an ambiguous lesson for Conservatives wedded to the belief that market forces are the most effective and efficient means of managing change. But they are also a challenge for Socialists. Interestingly, many of the most active local authorities in the new partnership arrangements with the private sector are traditionalist Labour authorities which have rejected the approach of their more 'radical' socialist colleagues, who have followed a socialized interventionist model of local economic development.

	Free-enterprise market model	Partnership model	Socialized collective economy model
Role of state actors	Minimalist	Joint public–private intervention	Public intervention and control
Policy instruments	Indirect, e.g. law Fiscal policy	Supportive services, e.g. small business advice, funding, training	Public agencies with direct controls over enterprise, e.g. planning agreements, enterprise boards
Policy objectives	To provide legal and fiscal framework to stimulate private enterprise	To provide range of partly subsidized services to stimulate new businesses	To plan for socialized economic growth and redistribute power in favour of organized labour and 'the disadvantaged'
Political ideology	'Conservative' Economic liberalism Capitalist economy	'Social democratic' Mixed-market economy	'Socialist' Socialized economy

Figure 4.2   The three competing models of local economic regeneration.

Thus, we have three main models of local economic regeneration, reflecting different political and economic orders. Given the intense interest across the party-political divide in local economic policies and regeneration, it is worthwhile outlining these different approaches (see Figure 4.2). Enterprise trusts, while supporting market-led regeneration, represent a form of partnership which is based on public-sector intervention directly and indirectly. A free-enterprise market model as an ideal type would not mobilize public resources in this way to assist firms directly. The state, at central and local level, would simply provide a legal and fiscal framework in which enterprise could work. In stark contrast, the socialized collectivist model would in theory include massive state intervention in and control over enterprise through such means as planning agreements, workers' control and direct equity investment in the private sector.

References

Birch, D. (1979), *The Job Generation Process* (Cambridge, Mass.: MIT).

Boyle, R. (1985), 'Symposium: "leveraging" urban development – a comparison of urban policy directions in the United States and Britain', *Policy and Politics*, vol. 13, no. 2, April, pp. 175–210.

Business in the Community (1985), '50,000 new jobs created a year', press release, 15 May (London: BIC).

Cawson, A. (1982), *Corporatism and Welfare: Social Policy and State Intervention in Britain* (London: Heinemann Educational).

Department of the Environment (1977), *Policy for the Inner Cities*, Cmnd 6845 (London: HMSO).

Fazey, I. H. (1987) *The Pathfinders* (London: Financial Training Publications).

Fothergill, S., and Gudgin, G. (1979), *The Job Generation Process in Britain*, Research Series No. 32 (London: Centre for Environmental Studies).

Hull, C. J. (with Hjern, B.) (1987), *Helping Small Firms Grow: An Implementation Approach* (London: Croom Helm).

McLennan, D., and Parr, J. (1979), *Regional Policy – Past Experience and New Directions* (Oxford: Martin Robertson).

Moore, C., and Booth, S. (1986a), 'From comprehensive regeneration to privatisation: the search for effective area strategies', in W. Lever and C. Moore (eds), *The City in Transition: Policies and Agencies for the Economic Regeneration of Clydeside* (Oxford: Oxford University Press), pp. 46–91.

Moore, C., and Booth, S. (1986b), 'Urban policy contradictions: the market versus redistributable approaches', *Policy and Politics*, vol. 14, No. 3, July, pp. 361–87.

Moore, C., and Booth, S. (1986c), 'The Scottish Development Agency: market consensus, public planning and local enterprise', *Local Economy*, no. 3, autumn, pp. 7–20.

Moore, C., and Booth, S. (1987), 'Regional economic development in the North East: critical lessons from Scotland', *Northern Economic Review*, winter, pp. 2–11.

Moore, C. and Booth, S. (1989) *Managing Competition: Corporatism, Pluralism and the Negotiated Order in Scotland* (Oxford: Oxford University Press).

Parkinson, M., and Duffy, J. (1984), 'Government's responses to inner city riots: the Minister for Merseyside and the task force', *Parliamentary Affairs*, no. 1, pp. 76–96.

Storey, D. (1982), *Entrepreneurship and the New Firm* (London: Croom Helm).

Storey, D., and Johnson, S. (1987), *Job Generation and Labour Market Change* (Basingstoke: Macmillan Education).

5 Evaluation of local responses

Introduction

As reported in Chapter 2, Layard and Nickell (1985) have estimated that 75 per cent of the increase in unemployment between 1975–9 and 1980–3 was the result of deficient demand. If we combine this view with analyses such as those by Gomulka (1979) and by the Brookings Institution (1980) cited in Chapter 1, then we may begin our approach to evaluating *local* responses with a degree of scepticism. What can be achieved when it is realized that at least 75 per cent of unemployment may be due to demand factors significantly beyond the influence of local communities and that there may well be some broad structural trends in the economy which neither national nor local governments can deal with easily. While it may be reasonable to argue that small *states* can, to some degree, withstand adverse international developments (Katzenstein 1985), it seems unlikely that local actors within national economies can withstand adverse national trends, unless regional economies are already to some degree independent of national economies, and unless local actors possess sufficient decision-making authority and resources of their own to introduce and implement distinctive policy programmes.

Since the UK economy is highly integrated, and the UK is a unitary and increasingly *centralized* state, it would be surprising if local actors – be they local or regional authorities, private firms, or new co-operative institutions such as enterprise trusts – could transform powerful national trends. This is not to deny the scope for some local action. The UK economy is centralized and highly integrated, but, as Moore and Booth (1989) argue with reference to Scotland, there are regions with some scope for distinctive industrial policy initiatives at the sectoral and enterprise level, through bodies such as the Scottish Development Agency. Even so, the problems confronting local agencies are enormous. If we take two fairly typical UK examples of industrial decline – steel and cars – it is clear that there are extremely powerful national and international forces at work which are difficult for the UK as a whole to resist, let alone for local communities, directly affected by the decline of these industries, to defeat.

In the case of the steel industry, its level of employment has declined from approximately 275,000 in the early 1970s to approximately 60,000 in 1988. Taking this industry alone, it would need a truly remarkable achievement on the part of local authorities and others in steel-making areas to create over 200,000 new jobs to replace those lost from the steel industry itself, let alone those lost in ancillary industries.

In the case of cars, the fact that the UK car market is now subject to import penetration of between 50 per cent and 60 per cent could hardly be altered significantly by the actions of local authorities or enterprise trusts in the West Midlands. As Spencer notes, manufacturing employment in the West Midlands fell by over 24 per cent between December 1979 and June 1982, producing a total loss of jobs (both manufacturing and other jobs) of 230,000 in just thirty months (Spencer, 1987). The decisions by, say, the Ford Motor Company or General Motors on whether to import models from West Germany, Belgium, or Italy are of far greater significance for levels of employment in the UK motor industry than the actions of any local agencies could hope to be.

Here, the key decisions will be taken in Detroit, rather than in Birmingham, Coventry, London, or even Brussels. Moreover, these decisions will be taken in the context of factors which are again outside local control – such as the state of labour relations, productivity trends, the quality of management training and indeed the general skills levels existing in nations. Key decisions can be (and have been) influenced by the actions of the UK *national* government – in 'persuading' Ford and General Motors to increase supplies from UK plants – but even there we see significant limitations. For example, import penetration reached 60 per cent of UK sales in August 1988, in part due to the decision by Ford to increase imports from its other European plants in order to meet a shortfall in UK production, caused by a strike in the UK plants earlier in the year. The decisions taken by local management regarding product design, price and reliability are equally impervious to local influence, even though these decisions are crucial – in the long run – to the local economies.

Neither economic nor political *power* resides at the regional or local level. Faced with this reality, it would be understandable if local responses had been few and far between. To some degree it might be argued that attempts by local communities to influence economic development are flying in the face of reality. Thus, in so far as success is achieved, is it a triumph of hope over 'reality' perhaps? Yet in practice, as we have seen, there has been a burgeoning of activity at the local level, greatly encouraged by national government. There has been no shortage of *activity* at this local level, as we have tried to show in earlier chapters. Our task, in this chapter, is to determine the *effects* of this activity.

Problems of evaluation: political motives and the absence of indicators?

Any evaluation of the impact of local responses takes place in the context of powerful broad national and regional trends. In early 1989, it happens that unemployment in the UK, however measured, is set on a clear downward path. Equally clearly, had we been writing this book some twenty years earlier, it would then have been evident that unemployment was still on a rising trend. Just as it would have been unfair to attribute the *rising* unemployment between 1974–5 and 1986–7 to the failure of local initiatives in coping with the problem, so it would be equally fallacious to attribute the current steady *fall* in unemployment to the effects of enterprise trusts, community business and local and regional subsidies.

The task of identifying causes and effects in this field is virtually impossible. This is in part because of the enormous dampening effects of national and international trends when set against any realistic estimate of what local communities can control and influence, but also because relatively little *evaluation* is attempted. This is perfectly consistent with the British approach to policy implementation and indeed may be a perfectly normal human reaction to situations which may be impossible to control in any immediate sense. Thus, 'doing something' or 'throwing money' at problems has both psychological and political benefits, even if it sometimes, or often, produces few tangible measurable benefits.

We will return in Chapter 6 to the *political* benefits of many of the local responses to unemployment, since we believe that these responses are best understood in relation to *system-maintaining* behaviour on the part of key actors, designed to accommodate and manage stressful (to the political system) issues which cannot be kept off the political agenda. That *political* motives and benefits are important is evident in the fact that the Conservative governments post-1979 have engaged in much intervention (and much public expenditure) while not really believing in it as effective solutions to economic problems. As the *Financial Times* commented:

> The Thatcher Government is sceptical of the merits of public-sector intervention in the economy. So it should not be too surprised that its policy of greatly increased assistance to small firms has been only a limited success . . . Schemes of this sort were introduced in the early 1980s as much for political as economic reasons. The Government wanted to be seen to be doing something about unemployment, which was then rising very rapidly.
>
> (*Financial Times*, 10 August 1988)

The relative lack of economic benefits, in contrast to the political benefits, of the government's assistance to small firms is evident in the report of the National Audit Office (NAO, 1988a). A number of worrying features were identified in the NAO's report. For example, the NAO examined the Enterprise Allowance Scheme (EAS), designed to help unemployed people who were to start a business, by paying them an allowance of £40 per week for a year. The payment is to remove the disincentive of giving up unemployment benefit or other income support, and currently costs the government approximately £200 million per year. Significantly, in terms of our thesis that in evaluating schemes we need to assess *political* as well as economic benefits, the NAO reported that '*the scheme has been, and remains, very successful in attracting people off the unemployment register into self-employment.* Over 300,000 people have come into the scheme since its inception in 1982' (NAO, 1988a, p. 1, our emphasis). Moreover, the net cost per person removed from the unemployment register was not high, at £2,300, and was broadly in line with other anti-unemployment schemes. Entry to the scheme was made as easy as possible, and there has been a steady rise in the number of participants – from 27,000 in 1983 to 106,000 in 1987–8 (see Table 5.1).

In terms of a simple objective of removing people from the unemployment register in a politically acceptable way and at reasonable financial cost, the scheme has been very successful. Other performance indicators present a less encouraging story, however. Thus, of the 222,900 people who entered EAS up to 31 March 1987, approximately 30,405 (13 per cent) left before completing the first year of the scheme. The drop-out rate has, in fact, been rising – from 13.5 per cent in 1983–4 to an estimated 16.0 per cent in 1987–8 – as

Table 5.1   Enterprise Allowance Scheme expenditure and entrants, 1982–3 to 1987–8

	Expenditure £m.	Target no. entrants	Entrants	Drop-outs[a]	Drop-out rate per cent
1982–3	2		2,500	365	14.6
1983–4	23	25,000	27,600	3,730	13.5
1984–5	77	50,000	46,000	5,060	11.0
1985–6	104	62,500	60,000	7,800	13.0
1986–7	143	85,900	86,800	13,450	15.5
1987–8	196	102,500	106,300	17,000	16.0[b]
Total	545		329,200	47,405	

[a] The drop-out figures relate to the batch of entrants in the previous column.
[b] Estimate.

Source: NAO, 1988a, p. 7.

more people have joined the scheme. The Department of Employment's own surveys reveal that 25 per cent of firms failed in the first six months after the allowance ended, and that 35 per cent had failed in the two years since the allowance ended. By taking into account the 13 per cent failure rate during the first twelve months of receiving the allowance, the NAO estimated that the survival rates at eighteen months and three years respectively are 66 per cent and 57 per cent (NAO, 1988a, p. 8).

The variety of business supported varies enormously (and includes busking!); but there is no evidence on whether survival rates are influenced by the *type* of business entered – again illustrating that evaluation is regarded as far less important than action in these anti-unemployment programmes. Indeed, the Department of Employment has actually rejected the notion of testing the viability of businesses, because of the costs of such an exercise, the inherent difficulty of picking winners and the possible deterrent effect on applicants.

The effects of the scheme in creating further jobs (i.e. in addition to removing one person from the unemployment register) are equally unencouraging. The Training Commission's follow-up surveys at eighteen months and three years suggest that about two-thirds of EAS businesses do not employ anyone (other than the recipient of the scheme), and that less than 4 per cent of them are responsible for more than 60 per cent of the new jobs created. At the three-year point the overall job-creation effect was 114 jobs (of which 30 were part-time) per 100 surviving firms (NAO, 1988a, p. 9). Further qualifications of the real effects of the scheme arise when 'deadweight' and 'displacement' effects are considered. It appears that 44 per cent of firms are in the 'deadweight' category, i.e. 44 per cent of firms would have started up in any case. The Department of Employment assumes that half of EAS businesses displace *existing* businesses and are *reducing* employment elsewhere. While recognizing the difficulty in verifying these figures (especially displacement figures), the NAO claims that deadweight and displacement estimates 'would reduce the job creation figures [i.e. 114 per 100 firms at the three-year point] considerably' (NAO, 1988a, p. 9).

The NAO's sober assessment of what the EAS actually achieves is in rather stark contrast to the government's *own* presentation of EAS. Thus, the Department of Employment's newspaper, *Employment News*, carried on its front page in August 1988 a report of the celebrations for the fifth anniversary of the EAS. In describing the 'bumper birthday bash' (which included a cake baked by Amanda Tidy, who opened Mandy's Bakery with the help of EAS), *Employment News* reported that 'since its launch the EAS has helped more than 350,000 people start their own business' and that 'the EAS also helps to create jobs – for every 100 businesses that are still trading three years after starting up, 114 additional jobs are created' (Department of Employment, 1988, p. 1). No mention was made either of the failure rate of the firms started by the 350,000 people who had passed through the scheme or of the deadweight and displacement effects cited above, despite the fact that the NAO's cautionary report had been published the previous month.

As the Director of the Hartlepool Enterprise Agency is reported as commenting, the EAS tends to produce too many odd-jobbers and hairdressers, attracted by the £40 per week allowance. Moreover, new EAS entrants begin to undercut last year's entrants, who no longer receive the £40 subsidy. As another respondent commented: 'If we are interested in net job creation, we don't really want to be helping to put the 500th mobile hairdresser in business so that they can knock out of the market someone whose £40 a week subsidy has now finished (both reported in the *Financial Times*, 15 March 1988).

The NAO's criticisms regarding EAS were broadly repeated in its review of the Loan Guarantee Scheme (LGS). Interestingly, there has been confusion over whether such a scheme was even necessary, with three separate committees producing different conclusions. Thus the Bolton Committee on Small Firms (1972) felt that the market was working effectively; the Wilson Committee (1980) felt that a scheme was necessary; and a later NEDO subcommittee investigated the issue and felt unable to give clear advice on the basis of the available evidence (NAO, 1988a, p. 10). Despite the lack of unambiguous evidence or advice, the Conservatives (notwithstanding their non-interventionist ideology) introduced a scheme in 1981. Failure rates on the scheme are assumed to be 30 per cent, and the intended self-financing of the scheme has not materialized. Thus, at March 1987 payments of £146 million had been made on called guarantees, against income of £37 million.

The lack of Conservative philosophy at the implementation level is further illustrated by the Department of Employment's response to the NAO's criticism that a comparison should be made between failure rates under LGS and failure rates on commercial lending. In reply, the Department of Employment did 'not consider that such comparisons are necessary for a justification of the scheme and believe[d] it should be judged by a comparison of its costs and benefits in terms of job creation and wealth creation' (NAO, 1988a, p. 13). Even the employment effects, however, have been difficult to estimate, because reliable and systematic data were not collected. What evidence there is suggests that job creation equalled 4.7 jobs per loan, but this includes no allowance for displacement. The NAO's attempt at a more sophisticated analysis of the available data produced a less encouraging result – namely, that the jobs created might be 3 per loan and that 36 per cent of the additional 836 jobs were generated by only eight firms (NAO, 1988a, p. 14).

Lack of proper evaluation was also highlighted by the NAO when it examined the Training for Enterprise programme (TFE), which is run by the Training Commission. This is yet another programme which has seen very rapid expansion under the 'non-interventionist' Conservatives: from 120 places in 1979–80 to 115,042 in 1987–8 (reflected in a costs increase from £0.4 million to £18.3 million in the same period). This growth has been 'strongly influenced by the government's support for creating an enterprise culture and the conviction that relevant training enhances the prospects of business success' (NAO, 1988a, p. 19).

Again we see what appears to be a 'gut reaction' to the unemployment problem, not necessarily supported by hard evidence of need and/or effectiveness. Thus, the NAO comments:

Replies to questionnaires by those completing training courses in 1986 have been generally favourable but NAO consider that *the performance indicators which the Training Commission uses may be*

> *misleading in giving credit to training for results which may be due to a variety of other factors, and in not taking account of deadweight.*
>
> (NAO, 1988a, p. 19, our emphasis)

A more general problem in evaluating the effectiveness of anti-unemployment schemes is that 'policy fashion' is a tremendously powerful driving force at the policy formulation stage, with no effective countervailing power base of scepticism on which a thorough programme of evaluation might be founded. In a related field – urban regeneration – the NAO has noted that the Department of the Environment did not specifically analyse the achievements and difficulties of the London Docklands Development Corporation or the Merseyside Development Corporation in order to identify any wider lessons before further Urban Development Corporations were established in 1987 and 1988 (NAO, 1988b, p. 5). The combination of 'policy fashions' with a natural desire to 'get things done' is a powerful source of policy innovation, if not of policy evaluation.

The push to get things moving was also evident in the Scottish Development Agency's approach. While generally praising the SDA's record in maximising private-sector involvement in its works, the NAO was critical of the SDA's monitoring arrangements (now improved) – particularly in cases being managed by the SDA's Property Development Division. Recognizing the difficulties in monitoring and assessing the wider development aspects of projects, the NAO nevertheless commented that 'in general there was very little information available on the performance of the projects in terms of the specific development gains identified in the original project appraisal' (NAO, 1988c, p. 13). In the case of the SDA's involvement in the Scottish Exhibition and Conference Centre, the NAO was critical of the relative lack of attention paid to the potential risks associated with the project or to the sensitivity of forecasts to different assumptions (NAO, 1988c, p. 16).

Finally, the NAO's report on arrangements for Regional Industrial Incentives (RIIs) provides further evidence that evaluation of effectiveness has proved elusive in practice and relatively unattractive, even for a government ostensibly committed to obtaining value for money in public expenditure and to shifting responsibility to the market where possible. The various departments involved in the RII scheme (the Department of Trade and Industry, the Scottish Office and the Welsh Office) told the NAO that they considered it inappropriate to set detailed programme objectives for RII because they were largely demand-led and were subject to external influences beyond departmental control. Moreover, they did not regard it as Government policy to conduct national planning in this way. *In these circumstances it was not surprising to find that there were few programme-related targets.*

(NAO, 1988d, p. 17, our emphasis)

This lack of enthusiasm for specifying programme-related targets occurs despite a developing governmental view that policies should in general contain clear, preferably quantified, objectives so that performance can be assessed (HM Treasury, 1987).

As always, the difficulty in setting targets is that non-achievement results in political as well as financial costs. The pattern is to conduct surveys of one kind or another which attempt to produce usable data and to assess recipient's responses to particular programmes. In the case of RIIs, available indicators produce mixed results. For example, there was no discernable effect on unemployment levels in Assisted Areas. In practice, there was no region where the unemployment trend appeared to be improved in Assisted Areas compared with unassisted areas in the same region. Indeed, in four of the eight regions, the trends appeared to be marginally worse, although other indicators produced a more optimistic evaluation (NAO, 1988d, pp. 17–21).

In essence, it has proved virtually impossible to devise any really meaningful assessment of the £400 million which the government was spending on RIIs in 1987–8 alone. It was not surprising, therefore, that in early 1988 the government announced a major reform of its regional policy, reflecting its own suspicions that Regional Development Grants often went to companies which would have made the investment without governmental assistance. However, Regional Selective Assistance has been retained, reflecting the government's view that inward investment must continue to be encouraged. Indeed, Lord Young, Secretary of State for Trade and Industry, has pledged that, *in total*, regional aid will not be cut, but that it will become more selective and more effectively targeted towards the expansion of small and medium-sized companies.

Doing good or feeling good? Local enterprise agencies and their achievements

If the National Audit Office – probably the greatest reservoir of evaluative expertise in the British system – has found difficulty in identifying reliable performance indicators for national programmes such as the EAS and RII schemes, we should perhaps be even more pessimistic about finding truly robust data on local enterprise agencies (LEAs) and other local initiatives. Without wishing to be as sceptical as the wag who, frustrated by the delay in the realization of grand plans to develop the 'Wonder World' recreation city on the site of Corby's former steel works, paint-sprayed 'Wonder when?' on the hoarding advertising the development, we need to follow the NAO's caution in assessing the rather bold claims made by proponents of the LEA 'solution'.

Before discussing the available data, however, it is important to emphasize the major importance of LEAs as a phenomenon of the 1980s. Of all the policy initiatives generated in response to the mass unemployment of the 1970s and 1980s, LEAs have proved to be the most broadly based in terms of political support. They are now to be found virtually everywhere in the UK and appear to be subject to little criticism. Like motherhood and apple pie, they are almost universally regarded as a 'good thing' and represent a classic example of a 'policy fashion' at work. We have seen a seemingly inexorable increase in the number of LEAs in the past few years, from an estimated 23 to over 250 in 1988. With Royal patronage – in the shape of active support from Prince Charles – it might be argued that LEAs are close to becoming a permanent feature of the policy landscape in the field of anti-unemployment and economic development policies.

In Chapters 3 and 4 we discussed both the organizational framework of local responses to unemployment and the actual policy responses, particularly in the areas which we selected for our case studies. We will discuss the possible achievements in the selected areas in the next section; but, before doing so, it is useful to refer to one of the few attempts to develop a *national* assessment of the LEA movement.

In 1986 Business in the Community (BIC) commissioned a firm of consultants, Enterprise Dynamics, to conduct a survey of LEAs in order to assess their contribution to the survival of small firms and to job creation generally. This report probably represents the most optimistic analysis of the effects of LEAs and is the most comprehensive source of systematic data available at present. As with the governmental programmes analysed by the NAO and cited above, LEAs put far more effort into *doing* than into *measuring*. For example, the survey found that there was no standard classification of an 'assisted client', and that some LEAs logged telephone calls to the agency in producing their record of assisted clients, while others counted only actual counselling of clients. Nevertheless, the survey of 114 agencies (81 of which returned the completed questionnaire) does present valuable data on the size and scope of LEAs and on their possible achievements. As always, assessment of performance depends upon the type of indicators selected. For example, 47 per cent of LEAs reported no change in unemployment in their areas since 1983, 30 per cent reported increases, and only 10 per cent reported a decrease (a further 13 per cent reported a 'change' but not the direction of the change) (BIC, 1987, p. 37).

The difficulty in isolating the specific contribution by the agencies themselves to solving the unemployment problem is illustrated by the fact that, in 40 per cent of the agencies, regional assistance was available to firms, while other forms of special assistance were available in 57 per cent of the agencies. A fifth of agencies had an Enterprise Zone in their area, and 59 per cent were within an area covered by COSFIRA (the Council for Small Firms in Rural Areas). In total, some twenty-eight different types of special assistance were mentioned as being available, ranging from the European Regional Development Fund to discretionary concessions on borough buildings.

Just as we argued that local responses to unemployment must be seen in the context of unemployment as a national problem, and in the context of the relatively weak powers devolved to localities in Britain (in contrast to Sweden, say – see Gustafsson, 1988), then so we must judge the *achievements* of LEAs and other local initiatives in the context of the large sums of public money available and the plethora of national schemes to assist firms and job creation. Indeed, a survey conducted by Ernst & Whinney, the accountancy firm, found that 60 per cent of businessmen wanted a cut in the number of grant schemes, to simplify the system (*Financial Times*, 14 January 1988). This does not mean that businessmen want reduced subsidies in total. For example, the House Builders' Federation produced a report in July 1988 which argued that the government's plans to attract greater private investment into the inner cities were doomed unless grants available to assist housing programmes in inner-city areas – currently costing the tax payer £400 million per year – were doubled to at least £800 million per year (HBF, 1988).

As we have argued elsewhere (Moore *et al.*, 1985), whatever is being achieved is being achieved in the context of nationally and locally funded public expenditure, albeit alongside private-sector money. An earlier survey by BIC suggested that the private sector was providing only 27 per cent of the *cash* resources of LEAs, with the rest being found through public expenditure (e.g. local and central government expenditure, the MSC and Urban Programme money), although the figure rose to 44 per cent when secondments and other business contributions were counted (BIC, 1986).

We also need to note the size of most LEAs. The 1986 survey indicated that LEAs were generally rather small, with an average full-time staff of 3.2 and an average part-time staff of 2.0, with over 90 per cent of the agencies having fewer than 5 full-time staff; only four of the surveyed agencies had more than 11 full-time staff (BIC, 1987, p. 47). The average core funding for the surveyed LEAs was £69,330, with only 29 per cent of LEAs with assured funding for more than one year. On average, each agency assisted 63 firms in 1981 and 315 firms in 1985 (excluding phone calls from the 'assisted firms' category).

The problems caused by the mismatch between 'doing' and 'evaluating' were also evident from the survey. Thus, *only twenty-four agencies supplied statistics identifying the numbers of surviving and defunct firms by year of assistance*. As a result, it was impossible to produce robust data on the survival rate of firms assisted by LEAs. The responses from the twenty-four agencies which supplied data suggest that approximately 20 per cent of firms assisted in 1984 and 1985 had ceased trading by 1986 (BIC, 1987, p. 45). Using all the available data, the results suggested that, over the survey sample as a whole, the failure rate for agency-assisted firms in the first three years is of the order of one in six.

This suggests, so the report argues, that 'Even when the results for the gloomiest years are examined, there seems little doubt that small firms assisted by enterprise agencies have a significantly better survival rate than the national average' (BIC, 1987, p. 75). Interestingly, the existence of family support was identified as of special importance, with significantly higher failure rates in those firms which lacked family support (22.1 per cent compared with 10.4 per cent). Perhaps neither of these statistics is surprising, in that it might be expected that firms which recognize that they need advice and actually seek it might be expected to produce better survival rates in any case. Similarly, if a budding entrepreneur lacks good family support, it is not surprising that he or she is likely to do less well.

The degree of contact between LEAs and client firms is also quite revealing of the scale of LEA activity. The majority of clients were in contact with the agencies three times or less, although there were considerable variations from agency to agency. In terms of services offered, the most widespread was enterprise training and other business education (see Table 5.2), even though enterprise training was mentioned by only one in ten firms (BIC, 1987, p. 103).

The importance of agency assistance to client firms was also assessed in the BIC survey. Some 94 per cent of firms said that they would have started *without* agency help, although 36 per cent said that the agency had helped them to get started more quickly (BIC, 1987, p. 107). Table 5.3 provides a breakdown of respondents' evaluation of agency help. In only 20 per cent of firms was the help thought to be crucial, although the average employment (5.8) and the net employment gain (2.1) were significantly high in such firms.

Finally, the BIC survey produced data on the extent of job creation in agency-assisted firms. The average employment per firm (including the owner) was 5.8, with a net gain of one job (equivalent full-time) per firm in 1986 (BIC, 1987, p. 10). If we use the BIC survey as the most reliable indicator of the achievement of LEAs in terms of job creation, then it is possible to produce a very rough estimate of the maximum total jobs created. Thus, if we assume that there were 260 agencies in 1988, and that the 1986 survey results of jobs created

Table 5.2   Agencies providing various small firm services

Type of service	Proportion providing service (%)
Enterprise training	59
Other business education	62
Small business club	57
Newsletter or newspaper	48
Involvement with workshop	40
Involvement with YTS	38
Other services	54

Note: Most agencies provide more than one of the above services, with the average figure being four. Ten per cent of agencies offer six or more of these services. Six per cent of agencies did not indicate whether they provided any of these services.

Source: BIC, 1987, p. 48.

Table 5.3   Importance of agency help

Classification	Proportion of firms	Proportion of employment	Average employment	Average net gain
Crucial	20	29	5.8	2.1
Useful	45	32	4.1	0.6
Marginal	27	21	4.3	0.2

Source: BIC, 1987, p. 105

per firm are accurate, then we can produce a gross employment-creation figure by multiplying the number of agencies (260, although the NAO estimated that 400 LEAs existed) by the average number of firms assisted by any one LEA (315 in 1985) in any one year – namely, 78,750 jobs created per year. This is a figure for jobs *associated* with enterprise trusts, rather than providing any direct correlation between number of firms helped, jobs created and agency intervention.

This calculation is in line with the estimate produced by BIC's Chief Executive, Stephen O'Brien, in January 1988, which suggested a figure of over 70,000 jobs per year (reported in the *Guardian*, 6 January 1988). More recently (in a paper, *The Future for Enterprise Agencies*, published by BIC in September 1988), reference was made to the studies conducted in 1985 and 1986 by the Centre for Employment Initiatives, which suggested that, overall, enterprise trusts were having an impact on approximately 90,000 jobs per year (BIC, 1988). If this is an accurate figure (but see below for criticisms of the validity of these estimates), then all LEAs in any one year will create somewhat in excess of the 40,000 mining jobs lost in Britain since the 1984–5 miners' strike.

As Mason has pointed out, even the most optimistic estimates of jobs created by initiatives in areas hard hit by massive redundancies are relatively small compared with the original job losses. Thus, he too notes that British Coal Enterprise claims to have created 5,700 jobs in its first year of operation, but that 40,000 jobs were lost from this industry after the miners' strike. Similarly, the total employment created in the Clyde Workshops, BSC (Industry)'s managed work-shop scheme, is equivalent to only one-fifth of the workforce in the steelworks in the mid-1970s (Mason, 1987, p. 387). The reason for this gross mismatch between initial redundancies and the eventual development of new firms is simple. As Mason points out, most of the new firms are extremely small. Thus, he quotes the case of the clients of the Business Link agency in Cheshire, 43 per cent of whom set up businesses employing only one person. He concludes: '*Indeed, few successful businesses with good long-term growth and job generation prospects have emerged from job creation initiatives*' (Mason, 1987, p. 307, our emphasis).

Mason goes on to examine the possible weaknesses in some of the job-creation claims being made. The problem of *additionality*, identified by the NAO in its report on national initiatives, is very important. As he suggests:

> because many sponsors of job creation initiatives do not take account of additionality, their claims about the number of jobs created or saved are likely to be inflated. Moreover, where a new or established small business has contacted two agencies for help, it is not unknown for *both* to include that firm in their 'jobs created' statistics.
>
> (Mason, 1987, p. 307)

The possibility of this double counting was also evident in BIC's 1987 report, in which 52 per cent of the agencies considered that their catchment area overlapped with that of another LEA, and 46 per cent of the agencies believed that firms used both LEAs. As the report admits: 'This suspicion was substantiated by a number of interviewed firms, some of whom reported that *in addition to consulting more than one agency, they had also done the rounds of other advisory bodies* such as, for example, the Welsh or Scottish Development Agencies' (BIC, 1987, p. 40, our emphasis). This is especially likely in some areas where the density of LEAs is now sufficiently high to suggest saturation point. For example, in Hartlepool there are two enterprise agencies and several other local support organisations.

Similarly, the *displacement* effect is identified by Mason as important because the vast majority of new businesses serve local markets. As we noted above, the EAS could in practice be displacing significant numbers of previous EAS recipients, as new, subsidized firms entered their markets. Mason also points out the problem of *targeting* assistance. Even where jobs are being created, they may not be going to the people who have been hit by large-scale redundancies. He cites the case of steel closures, where only 7 per cent of the businesses helped by BSC (I) are run by people with a steel-industry background (Mason, 1987, p. 307).

Neither do the statistics tell us much about the *quality* of jobs being created. For example, the *Financial Times*, in reviewing job-creation efforts in Hartlepool, reported that many of the new jobs created 'have been worth only £2 per hour and only women have been interested' (*Financial Times*, 15 March 1988). In fact, the differential between male and female unemployment rates in Hartlepool is startling (26.8 per cent and 11.4 per cent respectively), suggesting that job-creation efforts may be producing particular types of (often very low-paid or part-time) job, which in our present society are thought most suitable for women.

The overall picture that emerges appears to be one of much *activity*. For example, David Grayson, a Director of BIC, has suggested that 'enterprise agencies became the macho symbol of the 1980s . . . Every town had to have one' (*Financial Times*, 8 March 1988). This activity expresses an undoubtedly genuine concern by the private sector, voluntary bodies and local authorities to assist the regeneration of their communities. Equally, some of the job-creation figures, if taken at face value, would represent a significant and worthwhile achievement. On the other hand, as we and others have argued, the data are unreliable, and there is every reason to believe that the figures are an overestimate of the *tangible* achievements of LEAs and other local responses. (There are of course non-tangible achievements, which we discuss later in this chapter and in Chapter 6).

Despite these doubts, however, we have to recognize that thousands of individuals are making enormous efforts to encourage self-help in communities and in so doing draw upon whatever resources they can command – be they private or public. It would be both foolish and unjust to suggest that *nothing* worthwhile or tangible is being achieved on the ground at the local level. That much is indeed being achieved is evident from our own case studies, to which we now return briefly.

Local studies: practical programmes versus placebo responses

Even though BIC and the government itself are prepared to make claims about the number of jobs created, few local enterprise agencies or trusts would make strong claims about their impact on unemployment. As we have suggested, there are good reasons for being cautious.

Economic objectives can be ambiguous in theory and contradictory in practice. There is no simple correlation between job creation and reduced unemployment, because of the way in which labour markets operate across the spatial boundaries of initiatives and because of the variable capacity of individuals to compete successfully in the labour market. This has been one of the main lessons from the biggest urban renewal initiative in the UK, the Glasgow Eastern Area Renewal (GEAR) project (Moore and Booth, 1984). Indeed, employment might be viewed as only one measure of successful economic regeneration. Other indicators, including increased levels of investment in the local economy and the introduction of new technology in existing firms to make them more competitive, might be regarded as important long-term goals which could conflict with maximizing job creation.

Given this potential multiplicity of, and conflict between, objectives, evaluation is a problematical exercise. However, despite the aversion to jobs as the only criterion, it is undoubtedly the most politically salient measure and the central rationale for the new partnership movement in the local economy.

How can one assess the impact on jobs? There are three tests which can be applied, although in practice policy-makers and project managers tend to focus on the first. One test is the *quantitative* impact: how many jobs are being created or maintained by partnership intervention? Many enterprise trusts can give only a limited picture because they keep insufficient data. There are of course many extraneous influences on the activities of enterprise agencies, which makes them reluctant to put forward quantitative data. Measuring the net impact of any economic policy initiative, one is confronted by the problems of accounting for additionality and displacement, as we indicated above. In the case of enterprise trusts, the question is, how important was the support of the trust to the entrepreneur? In the case of a new business, the support of an enterprise trust may be very significant, although the BIC survey cited above suggested that this was true in only a minority of cases. Another influence might be in persuading an enterprise to locate in the local economy. However, the problem with counting for additionality is that it has to be set against a hypothetical scenario. We may be able to make some reasonable judgements. For example, if the rate of unemployment decreases beyond regional or national averages, we might infer *some* impact by local policy initiatives such as enterprise agencies. This seems to have been the case in Neath (see below).

Displacement is the impact on existing firms of supporting new businesses. A new enterprise may take sales and business away from established firms in the locality; and thus, while jobs may be being created in one enterprise, the net impact may not be that significant. For many enterprise trusts, the main client is the new small firm, often in the service sector, catering for a local market, as Mason (1987) and others have suggested. This could well mean a significant displacement impact. Where firms are 'exporting' goods and services or offering *new* goods and services in the local economy, the displacement impact will be less.

However, even if we could accurately account for these two factors of additionality and displacement, we cannot be certain that the development of an enterprise or jobs is specifically attributable to any one factor such as support from an enterprise agency. In many cases the agency is one element of a package of policies, including training and job creation grants, low cost premises and loans. The agency may have a legitimate claim concerning the jobs created as a result, but there is a need to have some such qualifications to the figures. Neath Partnership set itself targets by which to assess it activities. ENTRUST regularly reviewed its operations to produce some quantitative data on the results.

Unemployment and jobs created are only two indicators of impact and the state of the local economy, albeit the most politically salient measure. Making any judgements around these figures is notoriously difficult. First, the basis on which unemployment is calculated has changed over time. Secondly, the official statistics based on travel-to-work areas may not coincide with the boundaries of one enterprise agency. Thirdly, the 'job figures' produced by agencies may be subject to significant leakage. For example, Neath Partnership included employers' *potential* jobs figures as well as existing jobs to produce a figure of 1,700 jobs in firms assisted by the agency between 1982 and 1985. The St Helens Trust calculated that between 1977 and 1983 it had assisted in some 5,000 jobs. This figure was based on a 10 per cent survey of clients, grossed up. Similarly, ENTRUST calculated that it had assisted in stimulating or safeguarding 1,600 jobs between 1982 and 1984, based on a survey of clients which produced an 18 per cent response rate.

During the same period of time in which these assessments were being made by the individual agencies, what was happening to local employment? Table 5.4 gives us some idea for each initiative. It must be emphasized that the table is *not an attempt* to claim that one enterprise trust was more successful than another. Each agency must be looked at individually because of the different time periods involved, which meant that national, regional and local economic

Table 5.4 Relative performance of the partnership initiatives

Initiative	Assessment period	Number of jobs assessed by agency as associated with its intervention	Unemployment at start of period[a]			Unemployment at end of period[b]			Relative change		
			UK	Region	Area	UK	Region	Area	UK	Region	Area
NDP	1982–5	1,700[c]	3.063m. 13.2%	172,400 16.7%	4,421 16.4%	3.235m. 13.4%	176,500 16.6%	7,861 15.6%[d]	+0.2%	−0.1%	+3,440 −0.8%
St Helens	1977–83	5,000[e]	1.499m. 6.4%	215,900 7.7%	4,992 8.4%	3.084m. 12.9%.	436,700 15.7%	11,241 16.6%	+6.5%	+8%	+6,249 +8.2%
ENTRUST	1982–4	1,603[f]	3.063m. 13.2%	224,500 17.3%	93,317 16.6%	3.222m. 13.4%	238,900 18.7%	100.932 19.9%[g]	+0.2%	+1.4%	+7,615 +3.3%

a Unemployment at start of period. *Source:* Department of Employment, *Employment Gazette*, December 1977 (St Helens figures) and December 1982 (Neath and ENTRUST figures).

b Unemployment at end of period. *Source:* Department of Employment, *Employment Gazette*, December 1983 (St Helens figures), December 1984 (ENTRUST figures) and August 1985 (Neath figures). These dates approximately coincide with the period of assessment.

c *Source:* Neath Development Partnership Business Director's Report, August 1985. Calculated on employment associated with firms where NDP had a direct involvement and from information from those firms concerning potential jobs.

d The basis of the local area figures changed significantly during this period. In 1982 data were based on the Neath travel-to-work area. In 1985 data were based on the Neath and Port Talbot travel-to-work area.

e *Source:* survey of client firms conducted by St Helens Trust in 1983. This produced a 10 per cent response rate indicating a gross employment impact of up to 5,000 jobs over the period since 1977.

f *Source:* ENTRUST, *Annual Report*, 1985. Data based on a survey conducted for ENTRUST in 1985. A total of 1,250 questionnaires were sent out to clients, producing an 18 per cent response rate at the time of compiling the 1985 *Annual Report*. The jobs figure comprises new-start enterprises still trading, which employed 331 people, and established companies where jobs had been maintained or created, totalling 1,272 people.

g The local figures for the ENTRUST initiative are based on Tyne and Wear Metropolitan County Council, which corresponds to the main area of operation for the agency.

contexts were very different. For example, the figures for Neath clearly show that the worst of the recession and the manufacturing industry shake-out was over. In contrast, St Helens was in the midst of the recession and, in addition, suffered severe job losses in the glass industry. During the period Pilkington shed 3,000 jobs (Fazey, 1987), and other firms laid off around 12,000 people.

With this critical proviso, we can see that Neath appeared to perform very well in reversing unemployment in percentage terms, although the number of unemployed increased significantly. Much of this can be attributed to changes in the travel-to-work boundary during the period. If the calculation of 1,700 jobs is reasonably accurate for Neath, and unemployment increased in numerical terms by around 3,500, then we might argue that the Partnership helped slow down the increase in unemployment by about 50 per cent. In other words, assuming that the jobs are genuine new jobs being taken by people who would otherwise have been unemployed, unemployment in Neath in 1985 was 50 per cent less than it might have been without some such initiative as the Partnership.

The St Helens figures are clearly skewed by the recession nationally and redundancies in the glass industry, so that unemployment increased by 8.2 per cent or about 6,000 people between 1977 and 1983. If the job figures produced for the survey are to be believed, then unemployment would have been nearly twice as high. This may well exaggerate the impact of the Trust, since the data base is extremely tentative, but it does suggest a very significant impact despite the difficult economic conditions, although the unemployment levels continued to be very high.

Finally, in Newcastle there was an increase in numbers of unemployed between 1982 and 1984 of over 7,000, while the ENTRUST initiative was associated with 1,600 jobs. This indicates a relatively modest but again useful contribution to lessening the impact of unemployment in one of the UK's economically worst-hit areas in the past decade.

So we can make some tentative assessment of the impact of each individual initiative along this single dimension at these particular points in time, which suggests important contributions to stimulating enterprise and jobs. Without these initiatives, the figures for unemployment would have probably been worse, although not necessarily by the margins implied in the table, given the variable quality of the data. Of course, these crude figures take no account of additionality or displacement impacts. At the same time, the actual number unemployed has grown. This is not to say that the trusts have therefore failed, but only to say that their work must be seen in the context of what is happening in the local economy and to warn against expecting miracle results in terms of reversing job losses. The longer-term impact of the businesses being encouraged by the trusts *may* be even more significant. For example, the 'death rate' of new small firms in the UK nationally has been estimated at 40 per cent, while in St Helens it was calculated at 10 per cent. However, set against this is the problem of continuously stimulating investment in new start-up business. The 1987–8 *Annual Report* of the St Helens Trust reported that the number of new clients visiting the Trust declined over the year by 29 whilst the percentage of clients starting up in their own business was 18, lower than in the previous year (Community of St Helens Trust, 1988).

Indigenous jobs growth is a slow process. Fothergill and Gudgin (1979) calculated in a study of the Midlands that it would take anything up to ten years for new small firms to generate significant employment opportunities. Spencer's analysis of the West Midlands economy produced similarly pessimistic conclusions: 'even with the most favourable macro-economic policies and full Assisted Area status (not the present Selective Assistance status), the future of the region will remain rather bleak' (Spencer, 1987, p. 248). Other recent analysis has confirmed this argument (Curran, 1986; Doyle and Gallagher, 1986; Middleton and McEldowney, 1986).

We have discussed in some detail the quantitative impacts of the projects because this is the most politically important issue arising out of these initiatives. Whatever the limitations of the data, we can obtain some indication of what has happened in the localities over time and how this relates to the jobs generated through these projects. This gives us an idea of the *effectiveness* of enterprise agencies in helping to stimulate economic regeneration. Another way of assessing these initiatives is in terms of *efficiency*, relating input (in terms of the costs of running these agencies and money spent on supporting firms) to output (say, the number of jobs created or maintained).

Nationally, enterprise agencies are seen as very cost effective in terms of cost per job, especially in comparison to other policies such as regional aid. One analysis of regional aid indicates that, depending on the precise form of assistance given, the cost per job varied between £22,610 for selective aid up to £97,090 under the old regional employment premium (Moore, Rhodes and Taylor, 1986). In comparison, the Enterprise Allowance Scheme cost nearly £3,000 per job (*Employment Gazette*), 1984). Research done for Business in the Community indicated that an enterprise agency cost about £120 (1984 prices) per job created (Fazey, 1987). This suggests that enterprise trusts are a very cheap way of generating jobs.

This is somewhat misleading, however, since while the direct costs of supporting an agency are relatively low, often because firms second staff and give support in kind rather than cash, there may be considerable indirect costs. For example, in Neath significant funding for economic development was provided by public-sector agencies; and, in the case of MSC schemes, the Partnership enjoyed direct access to public funding. Similarly, Hamilton Enterprise Development Company (admittedly not quite the same as an enterprise trust) 'packaged' £5 million for local businesses in 1987–8 and had a further £15 million commited or in the pipeline, most of it public money. It was described by the *Financial Times* as 'essentially a channel for public sector funds' (*Financial Times*, 18 October 1988). In the same region, Joint Economic Initiatives (JEI), launched by Strathclyde Regional Council, is still reliant on public-sector agencies such as the SDA and the regional and district councils for most of its funding.

So cost per job, on the basis simply of how much it costs to run an enterprise agency, is not a true indication of efficiency. Enterprise agencies may be a relatively low-cost way of stimulating jobs, but, as we have emphasized, their task depends upon the availability of public funds, and their *total* impact remains problematic.

The above concerns the quantitative impacts. There is much less attention paid to two other critical measures associated with new employment: first, the *qualitative* impact, or what type of job opportunities are being encouraged? ·The qualitative dimension would include issues such as wages and general conditions of work, skill levels and the degree of part-time or casual employment. There is considerable political debate about this issue at national level. The Conservative government claims that the new 'enterprise culture' is creating new jobs, but opponents argue that these are low-paid, unskilled and often part-time opportunities which do not meet the needs of the bulk of the unemployed.

There are few systematic data at local level to assess these claims. Certainly, if one examines the type of enterprise which is being helped by individual agencies, there is a marked bias particularly towards new small businesses in the service sector, or in the light manufacturing sectors. Whether these jobs are considered qualitatively inferior to the old manufacturing jobs which they are replacing is partly a matter of subjective view, but some objective data could be generated in terms of such factors as wage levels. It is fairly clear, however, that the type of job being created is different and may not necessarily be suitable for those being laid off by the more traditional sectors, as was suggested in the case of areas affected by steel closures. The type of job being created reflects deeper structural shifts in the economy, to which enterprise agencies are responding.

This brings us to the third dimension of impact, namely, the *distributional* effect, or who gets what? At one level those benefiting from the new 'enterprise culture' in terms of jobs are not those who are being made unemployed. Research by Storey and Johnson (1987) found that as many as 45 per cent of new jobs could be part-time female employment, having relatively marginal impact on the existing unemployed. Similarly, McArthur (1985) found that employment opportunities being generated by special measures in Clydebank and the GEAR area of Glasgow were not reaching the unemployed. In a survey of 100 firms he found that only 20 per cent had been started up by someone who was previously unemployed, and very few of these could be classified as long-term unemployed. In addition, less than one-fifth of the entrepreneurs and less than half of their workers actually lived in the local communities, reflecting the openness of the labour market and the ability of new small firms to set themselves up where the incentives are best, and also illustrating the displacement potential of various schemes. McArthur observed: 'Unskilled adults and the long-term unemployed were conspicuously lacking among the 'enterprising unemployed'' (McArthur and McGregor, 1986, p. 132).

These findings should come as no real surprise. Labour markets do not function in isolation and rarely correspond to the spatial focus of particular initiatives. It is highly likely that people from outside the immediate area will benefit from the job opportunities, just as the residents of the locality may secure employment outside their place of residence. In some cases the fit may be much closer than in others. So, for example, town-wide initiatives may be more likely directly to benefit local entrepreneurs and the unemployed. Additional special measures may be necessary to enhance the competitiveness of local unemployed people to secure jobs. This was one of the lessons learned from the GEAR project in Glasgow, where the SDA introduced a special training and employment grants scheme to encourage local firms to take on locally unemployed residents and give them training (Moore and Booth, 1984). This scheme was subsequently extended to other SDA project areas.

Few enterprise agencies evaluate the distributional impact of their support for enterprise. Some engage in activities which target on locally unemployed people. NDP's extensive Community Programme and YTS agencies are good examples of this, and there is a specific attempt to link these places to longer-term employment opportunities. Clearly the analysis required in order to obtain a better idea of distributional impacts would be considerable. At the same time, enterprise agencies express an explicit concern with local unemployment. There is an assumption that by encouraging new economic activity locally, the benefits will filter down to the most disadvantaged people within the community. This is not a particularly sound assumption.

It is difficult to be precise about measuring impacts, especially in relation to jobs. Nevertheless, while we recognize that the jobs impact is not the only measure of success, and that in the short to medium term the number of jobs being generated is unlikely to match continued job losses, it is possible to argue that what we are seeing is a partially successful attack on the problem of unemployment by the enterprise agency initiative. This is the best that could be hoped for, given the influence of wider trends in the economy, structural shifts in employment patterns and the limited scope of the agencies themselves. The impact is in terms of marginal relative improvement or slowing down the rate of decline in the short to medium term. In the longer term it may be that the small enterprises of today will become the large employers of tomorrow, although existing research evidence is ambiguous. At the same time, a mixture of encouraging new small firms, helping to increase the competitive performance of existing enterprises, enhancing local training provision and improving the physical and psychological environment of communities can be viewed as a practical contribution to the process of transition.

In themselves, enterprise agencies can be only a partial response to decline and change, yet it seems that the hopes invested in them carry too much weight among some national politicians and business people. At another level, they do become a placebo if they are divorced from regional and national strategies or become in effect a substitute for action at these other levels. It is this level that we move into the realms of ideology or the underlying values of this form of policy intervention, to which we turn in Chapter 6.

Non-measurable benefits

Supporters and participants in the enterprise trust movement may well object to our crude attempt to measure performance. As we ourselves admit, performance measurement is fraught with difficulties, which in part explains the relative lack of effort being put into evaluation compared to the effort invested in action.

In many ways LEAs are now at at a turning point in their history The desperation of the late 1970s and early 1980s, caused by the then seemingly inexorable rise in unemployment, which gave birth to the LEA movement, has been replaced by a national concern for an overheated and booming economy. The danger for the still very large numbers of people unemployed is that the *political* motivation for developing effective solutions may well decline. As one key figure in the development of the trust movement commented in 1982:

> If one views the present recession as simply a cyclical phenomenon, then one can look forward to a time when we will all go back to the conditions of the late 70s . . . If this is the case, then it is difficult to see that Enterprise Trusts or Agencies have any future, beyond the short-term assistance of small and new businesses through a difficult period of economic history.
>
> (Humphrey, 1982, pp. 7–8)

Like most movements, the LEA movement started in response to a new problem faced by society at a time when many had begun to question the old ways of problem-solving in general. Thus, mass unemployment arose at a time when centralized large-scale solutions were beginning to be questioned as responses to societal problems. LEAs were 'conceived outside any hierarchy and from the bottom up . . . They were community based with the concept of a community pulling itself up by its own bootstraps and not relying on "them" to provide the answer' (Humphrey, 1982, p. 2). Although we would question the independence from 'them' (in that public expenditure has been crucial to the development and work of LEAs), there is no doubt that LEAs are a good example of the new ideology of self-help which has emerged in the 1980s. Equally, there is no doubt that LEAs have achieved an important *status* in the system. As Humphrey observes, the initial problem was credibility, whereas by 1982 '. . . everyone applauds the concept of an Enterprise Trust, and both public and private sector support is taken for granted (Humphrey, 1982, p. 2).

Trusts are a well-established part of the policy machinery – as indicated by limited government funding for LEAs, via the Department of Employment's Regional Enterprise Units administering the Local Enterprise Agency Grant Scheme (LEAGS). (The scheme cost £2.3 million in 1986–7.) The movement now has to decide on how to build upon existing achievements and how to develop a new phase of assistance to firms. A key question to be resolved in this process is the funding of LEAs and their independence from central government. At present, LEAs appear not to have achieved the independence from 'them' suggested by Humphrey as part of the motivation for LEAs. Thus, the NAO reports that comments from The Regional Enterprise Units of the Department of Employment suggest that some agencies would not survive without LEAGS. It was clear to the NAO '. . . that a large proportion of LEAGS-assisted agencies rely heavily on the grant schemes, local authority support and money from a small number of private sector sponsors, usually large national concerns' (NAO, 1988a, pp. 21–2). This suggests that the government's intention to run LEAGS for five years and no more may be difficult to achieve if the movement is to continue.

Whether the movement withers (if the economy continues to improve), or whether it develops a different set of objectives – beyond the preoccupation with helping new and small firms – depends upon evaluation of what has been achieved so far. One difficulty is that those involved in LEAs would probably reject our approach of trying to find tangible and measurable benefits *now*. Much of the rationale of LEAs, they would argue, is to change attitudes and behaviour in the long term. Results can only be assessed over ten or twenty years, according to this philosophy. In theory, this is perfectly reasonable, since it is only when small businesses, become medium sized that employment generation really takes off. Moreover, they would argue, the most dynamic economies are those with thriving small and medium-sided firm sectors. Reliance on 'mature' and large corporations leads to sluggish innovation and growth. In terms of long-term growth in the economy, then, *any* help to the development of small firms must be good, even if it produces few net jobs in the short run, when measured against the scale of current redundancies.

Thus, in judging the performance of, say, the St Helens Trust, we should accept that the Trust could never hope to counteract the scale of redundancies in the town. These have been over 20,000 in ten years, with both Pilkington and United Glass shedding over half of their workforce in this period, and five of the original eight firms which were approached to help form the Trust having closed. The Trust's philosophy is to create the seed-bed for economic activity in the future although as indicated earlier this may become an increasingly difficult task given the limit on potential entrepreneurs and new activities in the local economy. By definition, we can assess the Trust's achievement only when sufficient time has passed for the seeds to have grown. As Mason suggests, in the long-term '. . . such initiatives might help to stimulate a local enterprise culture by highlighting the scope for entrepreneurial activity' (Mason, 1987, p. 308). Mason also emphasized the *symbolic* importance of the activity – a factor on which we ourselves place the greatest emphasis. Thus, in the short term

> the symbolic value of corporate job creation initiatives and the rapid growth achieved by some new companies which such initiatives have assisted . . . can be of great importance in increasing hope, morale and confidence, *all* commodities that are scarce in communities suffering from the erosion of their employment base.
>
> (Mason, 1987, p. 308)

Perhaps the key to the performance of LEAs, beyond this socio-political role, is the degree to which they can become proactive, rather than reactive. Evidence from a statistical study of the factors which influence the growth of small firms in West Germany suggests that the existence of effective intermediaries, to which firms can turn, can have a very marked effect on local economic performance.

Thus, in a study of four localities, Hull found that in Borken growth rates were much higher than elsewhere, largely because of the effectiveness of intermediaries to which firms could turn for help (Hull with Hjern, 1987. Of particular significance for the future development of the LEA movement in Britain, Hull and Hjern's findings suggested that the Borken County Economic Development Agency '. . . positively influenced employment in more troubled firms, but by helping to secure existing rather than [adding] new jobs' (Hull with Hjern, 1987, p. 139). They conclude that, if the aim is to exploit employment potential to the full, 'resource identification and problem definition may be necessary. Borken's Economic Development Agency appears to achieve this' (Hull with Hjern, 1987, p. 144). Emphasizing the importance of intermediaries to which small firms can turn, they conclude that the intermediary *par excellence* in Borken is the Economic Development Agency: 'The Agency brings a large number of firms with many kinds of problem into contact with a range of resources and institutions, and it combines this breadth of assistance with functional depth' (Hull with Hjern, 1987, p. 152).

The key factor in this analysis is the importance of *intermediation*. In essence, all modern states have developed complex assistance structures and programmes for small firms. The 'trick' is successfully to link firms to those structures which can provide the firm with the necessary resources for growth. Diagramatically, Hull depicts two situations: one where firms with a need for assistance in problem definition (PD), resource identification (RI) and resource mobilization (RM) do not connect effectively with the resource providers (be they banks, governments, or other agencies); and one where there is effective 'intermediation' (see Figure 5.1).

Comparison between the UK and West German situations presents difficulties, of course. For example, the Economic Development Agency in Borken cannot be compared with LEAs in terms of its composition and status. Thus the agency is not quite the same as the public–private mix of UK LEAs. It is a 'private-law' agency whose shareholders are the county governments in its constituent local authorities, rather than a public–private partnership. But its key

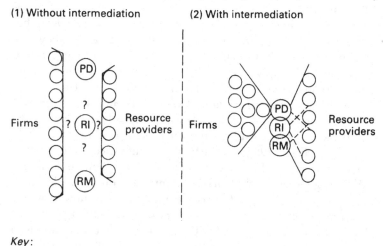

(1) Without intermediation　　**(2) With intermediation**

Firms　Resource providers　|　Firms　Resource providers

Key:

PD　　Problem definition
RI　　Resource indentification
RM　　Resource mobilization

Figure 5.1　Linkage between firms and resource providers – extreme cases.

Source: Hull with Hjern, 1987, p. 11.

feature is akin to those of LEAs in Britain, namely, the agency's 'half-in, half-out' status, which enables it to act as a very effective intermediary between local authorities and other levels of government and the firms themselves. Moreover, it has added a range of attributes which make it uniquely effective in this intermediary role, namely, 'the extent of its outreach to firms; the breadth of problem coverage which it provides; the depth of its assistance in terms of problem definition, resource identification and mobilization, and the intensity of its contacts with resource-providing sectors' (Hull with Hjern, 1987, p. 173).

Moon and Willoughby (1988) have also drawn attention to the same factors in their study of one of the leading Australian examples of the local generation of new enterprises. Using the concept of 'facilitators' they conclude that the work of 'facilitators' is characterized by 'a people-centred analytic approach (no formulas for local enterprise development); "policy entrepreneurship" in the use of government resources; and a networking mode of operation at the local, state and national levels'.

We might conclude by suggesting that the empirical evidence in the UK is that there is plenty of *demand* for what Hull has called intermediaries (Hull with Hjern, 1987), or what Moon and Willoughby (1988) call facilitators, and that LEAs have clearly (as witnessed by their sheer survival and growth) begun to meet some of that demand. As the prime motivation – mass and rising unemployment – may have declined in importance, and as direct government funding is phased out, the LEAs will need to develop the kind of professionalism which Hull cites as the key to the success of Borken's Economic Development Agency. Whether LEAs can do this depends greatly upon the initiative of the *private* sector in Britain. Our concluding chapter therefore now turns to the broader political forces at work in shaping and guiding this private-sector participation in local partnership schemes, because this now seems central to the future development of both national and local responses to unemployment and to local attempts at economic regeneration.

References

Bolton Committee (1971), *Report of the Committee of Inquiry on Small Firms,* Cmnd 4811 (London: HMSO).
Brookings Institution (1980), *Britain's Economic Performance* (Washington, DC: Brookings Institution).

Business in the Community (1986), *Survey of Local Enterprise Agencies* (London: BIC).

BIC (1987), *Small Firms and Job Creation: The Contribution of Enterprise Agencies* (London: BIC).

BIC (1988), *The Future for Enterprise Agencies* (London: BIC).

Community of St Helens Trust (1988) *Annual Report* (St Helens: Community of St Helens Trust).

Curran, J. (1986), *Bolton Fifteen Years On* (London: Small Business Research Trust).

Department of Employment (1988), *Employment News*, no. 167, August.

Doyle, J., and Gallagher, C. (1986), *Size Distribution Potential for Growth and Contribution to Job Generation of Firms in the UK 1982–84*, Research Report No. 7 (Newcastle: Department of Industrial Management, University of Newcastle upon Tyne).

Fazey, I. H. (1987), *The Pathfinders* (London: Financial Training Publications).

Fothergill, S. and Gudgin, G. (1979), *The Job Generation Process in Britain*, Research Series No. 32 (London: Centre for Environmental Studies).

Gomulka, S. (1979), 'Britain's slow industrial growth – increasing efficiency versus low rate of technical change', in W. Beckerman (ed.), *Slow Growth in Britain. Consensus and Consequences* (Oxford: Oxford University Press).

Gustafsson, G. (1988), 'Challenges confronting Swedish decision-makers: political and policy responses, 1974–1986', in E. Damgaard, P. Gerlich and J. J. Richardson (eds), *The Politics of Economic Crises: Lessons from Western Europe* (London: Sage).

HM Treasury (1987), *Treasury Minute*, CM 36.

House Builders' Federation (1988), *Private House Building in the Inner Cities* (London: HBF).

Hull, C. J., with Hjern, B. (1987), *Helping Small Firms Grow: An Implementation Approach* (London: Croom Helm).

Humphrey, W. E. G. (1982), 'Enterprise trusts: looking back and looking forward', unpublished paper.

Katzenstein, P. (1985), *Small States in World Markets* (Ithaca, NY; and London: Cornell University Press).

Layard, P., and Nickell, S. (1985), 'The causes of British unemployment', *National Institute Economic review*, no. 11, February.

McArthur, A. (1985), *Local Economic Regeneration: Community Level Effects in Clydeside*, Discussion Paper No. 16 (Glasgow: Centre for Urban and Regional Research, University of Glasgow).

McArthur, A., and McGregor, A. (1986), 'Policies for the disadvantaged in the labour market', in W. Lever and C. Moore (eds), *The City in Transition: Policies and Agencies for the Economic Regeneration of Clydeside* (Oxford: Oxford University Press), pp. 120–41.

Mason, C. (1987), 'Job creation initiatives in the UK: the large company role', *Industrial Relations Journal*, vol. 18, no. 4, pp. 298–311.

Middleton, A., and McEldowney, J. (1986), 'Small-scale economic activity and regional decline in Northern Ireland and Strathclyde', occasional paper, Department of Urban Design and Regional Planning, Edinburgh University.

Moon, J. W., and Willoughby, K. W. (1988), *An Evaluation of Local Enterprise Initiatives: The Case of Esperance* (Perth, WA: Office of Local Government, Department of Regional Development and the Northwest).

Moore, C., and Booth, S. (1984), *Urban Economic Adjustment and Regeneration: The Role of the Scottish Development Agency*, ESRC Inner Cities in Context Project, Working Paper No. 10 (Glasgow: University of Glasgow).

Moore, C., and Booth, S. (1989), *Managing Competition: Meso-Corporatism, Pluralism and the Negotiated Order in Scotland* (Oxford: Oxford University Press).

Moore, C., Moon, J. W., and Richardson, J. J. (1985), 'New partnerships in Local Economic Development. A case study of local entrepreneurship,' *Local Government Studies*, Vol. II, No 5, pp. 19–34.

Moore, C., Rhodes, J., and Taylor, I. (1986), *The Effects of Government Regional Economic Policy* (London: HMSO).

National Audit Office (1988a), *Department of Employment/Training Commission: Assistance to Small Firms* HC 655.

NAO (1988b), *Department of the Environment: Urban Development Corporation*, HC 492.

NAO (1988c), *Scottish Development Agency: Involvement with the Private Sector*, HC 478.

NAO (1988d), *Department of Trade and Industry, Scottish Office and Welsh Office: Arrangements for Regional Industrial Incentives*, HC 346.

Spencer, K. (1987), 'The West Midlands: an economy in crisis', in V. Hausner (ed.), *Urban Economic Change: Five City Studies* (Oxford: Oxford University Press).

Storey, D., and Johnson, S. (1987), *Job Generation and Labour Market Change* (Basingstoke: Macmillan Education).

Wilson Committee (1980), *Report of the Committee to Review the Functioning of Financial Institutions*, Cmnd 7937 (London: HMSO).

6 The private sector comes to town: effective solutions or political management

Introduction

Much of our argument has been couched in what some may see as rather sceptical terms. This may have seemed churlish when what we are examining in this book are the enormous and genuine efforts made by local communities, in the form of partnerships between the public and private sectors, to combat rising unemployment and accelerating economic decline. We have adopted a critical approach to the analysis of achievement because we too share the same concerns for devastated communities in Britain. Whether one believes that the trauma that the British economy has gone through since the oil shock of 1974/5 has been necessary in order to achieve a stronger and more efficient economy, or whether one believes that much of the agony could have been avoided by the use of more interventionist policies, one cannot but recognize that countless citizens have been innocent victims of economic forces beyond their control. But caring must be matched by a realistic assessment of what the practical actions of those involved actually achieve. We recognize that measuring these effects is extremely difficult – in part because of technical problems such as additionality and displacement, but also because the benefits of action may be visible only in the long-term. Another reason, which we will concentrate on in this concluding chapter, is that some of the effects (perhaps the most important ones) are not to be seen in numbers or quality of jobs created, but in broader political, social and possibly ideological terms.

It may be reasonable to argue that the phenomenon that we have described in this book – namely, the emergence of a new spirit of *partnership* at the local level – may be a purely temporary one, albeit very necessary, while broader structural changes in the economy work themselves through and the economy finds a new equilibrium based upon a different structure and distribution of costs and benefits. That Britain may, indeed, have been passing through a major (and arguably 'natural') transition of its economy is given some support by Harold Wolman's comparative analysis of urban economic performance. Thus, he found that 'the difference among areas in the performance of their manufacturing sector had a greater impact on differentiating between good and poor economic performers than differences in service performance'. This, he suggests, may mean that

> the gulf between good and poor performers may lessen as the run-down in manufacturing employment finally comes to a halt. Thus, if the problem is seen as the *extent of variation* in the performance of Britain's urban economies and the size of the gulf between good and poor performers, there is good reason to believe that, even without effective policy intervention, the variation and gulf are likely to diminish over time.
>
> (Wolman, 1987, pp. 37–8)

Wolman's well-researched study produced some particularly worrying data for Britain. For example, the finding that differences in economic performance of urban areas in recent decades were *not* related to degrees of success in gaining employment in the rapidly growing service sectors was particularly true for the UK when compared with West Germany and the USA. He found that in Britain there was only a 3.9 per cent difference in service-sector growth between good performers and poor performers, but that there was a 23.6 per cent difference in employment change in the manufacturing sector (Wolman, 1987, pp. 25–6). His findings over time are, in fact, quite startling. Thus, between 1971 and 1981 the good performers *increased* their employment by 8.11 per cent while the poor performers saw a *decrease* in employment of 7.40 per cent, showing a difference of 15.5 per cent between the good and bad performers, with *threequarters* of that difference due to performance in the manufacturing sector and only one-fifth due to service-sector performance (Wolman, 1987, p. 26).

National trends appear to be important. For example, overall manufacturing employment in Britain declined by 24 per cent in the 1970s compared with an increase for the USA of 5 per cent. Even the growth in Britain's service sector compared unfavourably, in that Britain's service sector grew by only 22 per cent compared with

41.4 per cent for the USA (Wolman, 1987, p. 28). Wolman's findings, based on an analysis of urban and regional economies, seem consistent with the findings of organizations like the Brookings Institution (cited in Chapter 5) which suggest that a major element in Britain's decline is some national traits which relate to productivity, rates of innovation and broad cultural attitudes. Further evidence of *national* factors also came from Wolman's research – namely, that 'good urban economic performance was related to labour-force skill and education levels'; this, he suggests, indicates that there is a 'need for greater emphasis on improved access to higher education and vocational training for the general work-force – an area in which Britain lags badly behind the USA and Germany' (Wolman, 1987, p. 38).

The link between training and economic development was also emphasized by McArthur and McGregor in their study of local employment and training initiatives in Britain. They argued that 'if government were to afford local authorities more legislative powers to intervene in local labour markets, as it has done in the area of local economic development, the potential for local authority action would be markedly improved' (McArthur and McGregor, 1987, p. 150). As it is, local authorities are constrained both by statute and expenditure restrictions and cannot, therefore, develop really effective local labour market strategies.

Here, then, we have two studies which to some degree highlight the importance of factors which may be beyond the control of local actors in Britain. Yet we have seen, particularly since the Conservatives were elected in 1979, a policy mix which is a strange amalgam of tough national policies which undoubtedly exacerbated the unemployment problem, if only in the short term, combined with active national encouragement of local initiatives based upon the principle of self-help, even though the government itself was responsible for the increasing *centralization* of decision-making in Britain (Richardson, 1988) We are, therefore, faced with apparently contradictory trends in Britain: policies pursued by national governments which appear to accelerate the decline of the manufacturing sector; an intensification of a trend, already established under Labour, towards much greater control over local government; and clear attempts to devolve responsibility for difficult problems, such as unemployment, to the periphery. Such contradictions are not unusual; but even so, we need to be aware of their policy consequences. As Rhodes has suggested, there are 'feedback effects' related to the different trends. Citing the example of expenditure controls on local authorities, he argues: 'expenditure controls fell largely on local capital expenditure and, in effect, off-loaded public sector cuts on to the private sector, e.g. the construction industry. This simply contributed to the de-industrialization of the British economy and rising unemployment. Government action was intensifying economic decline' (Rhodes, 1988, p. 385). Without our wishing to comment on whether the attempts to restrict local authority expenditure were necessary or not, Rhodes's example does illustrate the complexity of the policy mix in operation. Yet it is possible to make sense of these apparently contradictory trends – but not in terms of conventional indicators of policy performance. Sense can only be made of these many developments by addressing broader political and ideological factors, to which we now turn.

Partnership: corporate motives, costs and benefits

Local authority interest in local economies is not new. The 1970s and 1980s saw the *intensification* of that interest and an increase in the rate of policy innovation by local authorities. What is possibly new, as Chandler and Lawless note, is the *conscious* creation of new employment by local authorities. Thus, they cite a survey by the Association of District Councils in 1980 which stated that 'support and development of the local economy [are] now a top priority for almost every local authority' (Chandler and Lawless, 1985, p. 3). In fact, even this very particular concern is not new. As Mawson and Miller note: 'local authority intervention in the local economy has a long history stretching back well before the emergence of central government's regional policy in the 1930s. This tradition reflected the view that there was a legitimate role for local government to play in helping the unemployed directly and in undertaking measures to foster business development' (Mawson and Miller, 1987, p. 188). What we have seen in the 1970s and 1980s is the emergence of a few 'interventionist' authorities, born of ideas developed within the labour movement and reflecting a fairly wide view of what the agenda should be – including distributional issues, questions of access and opportunity and what are seen as aritificial distinctions between economic and social policy issues (Mawson and Miller, 1987, p. 194).

While the 'interventionist' authorities like Sheffield, with its Employment Department, and the West Midlands, with its West

Midlands Enterprise Board, have gained much more publicity and national attention, the mainstream of local authorities have not gone down the route of challenging the prevailing ideology, even though they reject the government's economic and labour market policies. If one word is used to characterize the *predominant* local response, it is 'partnership' rather than 'intervention'. Moreover, 'partnership' is a more appropriate label in other policy areas, too – such as education and urban renewal – than is 'intervention', even though, as we have argued in earlier chapters, partnership is invariably exercised in the context of increased public expenditure. The really *new* development, therefore, is the widespread involvement of the private sector in response to such national issues as unemployment, urban decay and even education at all levels, from the involvement of companies in the new City Technology Colleges, to a greater role being granted to private industry in the running of the universities via the new University Funding Council. Space does not permit an examination of increased private-sector influence and involvement in these other policy areas (which include even the arts) but we draw attention to these developments because they appear to be related to a more widespread and potentially powerful development – namely, that of increased corporate involvement in public and social issues. While the majority of local authorities have failed to escape the constitutional and political constraints placed upon their actions, business has begun to make what may turn out to be a fundamental shift in its role in society.

Increased private-sector involvement via the developing sense of corporate responsibility in Britain is, of course, set in the context of a system of business–government relations in which there has been traditionally a close relationship between the public and private domains. As Antal suggests, we need to understand the socio-political environment, as well as the organizational culture of particularly businesses, in order to understand the way that corporate social responsibility is shaped. Thus, the socio-political environment both influences the agenda of issues and problems, and influences what business is expected to do (Antal, 1985, p. 232). Vogel notes that British business people exhibit a set of values and beliefs which may make them less suspicious of government and state than their US counterparts might be. He argues that 'ironically, while the ideology of corporate social responsibility is far more widespread in the United States than it is in Great Britain, the practices of British business actually appear to conform much more closely to its ideals'

(Vogel, 1986, p. 250). The norms under which business operates in Britain make it 'more susceptible to social pressure from both government officials and other firms to behave "responsibly" ' (Vogel, 1986, p. 250).

There are certainly developing pressures for British business to become more systematic in developing its corporate social responsibility more actively. In part, the pressure has come from existing business organizations themselves. For example, the CBI has increasingly assumed responsibility for advancing and implementing public programmes through its participation in the Training Commission (formerly the MSC) and through its own policy initiatives, such as the creation of its Urban Regeneration Task Force, which published its report, *Initiatives Beyond Charity*, in September 1988 (CBI, 1988; see below). The origins of BIC and other organizations were mentioned in Chapter 3, and it is now estimated that business support for LEAs is in excess of £30 million per year.

Peer-group pressure has also been an important aspect of encouraging a growing corporate responsiveness to those social issues. For example, Prince Charles (who is President of BIC) has argued that 'it is necessary to try and achieve a more enthusiastic response from the private sector towards the needs of each local community and the community in which each company business is located' (BIC, 1986, p. 4). Similarly, Robin Leigh-Pemberton, Governor of the Bank of England, has called for a major initiative by companies to reverse the 'misery and alienation' within Britain's inner cities. Echoing Prince Charles's call for more involvement, he argued that it was 'perfectly appropriate that commercial companies should develop a definite policy in respect of their social responsibility in the areas in which they operate '(BIC, 1986, p. 5).

The collective peer-group pressure to which Vogel refers is evidenced by the behaviour of the CBI, which, for example, set up a Community Task Force, following an approach from the government in early 1985, designed to increase awareness of the government's Community Programme and to encourage experimentation and greater involvement by industry. The Task Force made specific proposals to the government for an improvement in the operation of the Community Programme and was given permission to set up twenty experimental projects. Thus, in some respects at least, the CBI has reached stage three of Ackerman's model of the development of social responsiveness; i.e. it has passed through stage one (the establishment of a commitment to respond to an issue) and stage two (the acquisition of specialized knowledge or skills to deal with it) and is now in stage three, the implementation of the response and its integration into standard operating procedures (Ackerman, 1975). Thus, there are sufficient indicators of change to suggest that British business may belatedly be moving in the same direction as that in which US business moved in the 1960s and 1970s.

Corporate responsibility is fundamentally about the relationship between business and society, and in particular between big business and society. The classical school of liberal economic theory based on the 'free market' philosophy sees the company purely as an *economic agent*. In this conception the corporation meets its social responsibilities by maximizing profits and operating efficiently in responding to the market. The whole idea of any wider corporate social responsibility is contrary to the principles of a free market and contrary to the interests of shareholders and employees. Under this model, we would not expect business to be involved in the creation, funding and running of LEAs, for example.

This view is criticized by those who see the corporation as a *social organization*. They argue that the liberal market approach ignores key developments in the modern business corporation, which exercise considerable influence over the working of the market. Firms are as interested in goals of steady growth and stability as in profit maximization and risk. These interests lead to an interdependency with government intervention in the economy and to the gradual involvement of business in community affairs which have no apparent *direct* link with business profits. Yet, in essence, this involvement is often defended in terms of self-interest. As Lord Carr, Chairman of the Prudential Assurance Society and Chairman of BIC, put it: 'the commercial success of business organizations is affected by the health and prosperity of society, and especially by the health and prosperity of the communities where they produce or sell their goods and services' (BIC, 1986, p. 8). This conception raises questions about the political and social powers and the role of the modern corporation.

Other observers have linked the market responsiveness and commercial operation of business with a capacity of the corporation to meet social objectives. For example, Drucker has referred to the 'third' or 'mixed' sector, comprising non-governmental institutions serving public policy goals. This sector could include the business corporation acting either directly or in partnership with other organizations to deliver social programmes as defined by government and with some public funding (Drucker, 1984). Discussing the provision of social welfare benefits, Rein argues that the conventional dichotomy between the public and private sector is misleading (Rein, 1982). He suggests that the established category of the 'welfare state', meaning essentially government or public services and transfer payments, does not adequately reflect the extent of social provision in modern industrial economies and the complex intermeshing of public and private contributions. In his view it is more accurate to talk of the 'welfare economy', which takes into account the variety of institutional forms by which society carries out the welfare function. The growth of fringe benefits has been marked in all Western economies, and Rein suggests that the more recent general governmental strategies of cutting public expenditure and reducing the role of the state will lead to even greater emphasis on the private sector as the institutional mechanism of social welfare delivery. There is plenty of evidence of this trend in Britain, as we have indicated above in referring to developments in such diverse sectors as urban renewal, education policy and funding of the arts.

Smith talks of the 'new political economy' and the 'contract state' in the USA, while in Britain the emphasis has been on the growth of quasi-governmental and non-governmental bodies (Smith, 1975). The present Conservative government has sought to reduce this form of indirect administration as much as it has the more direct forms of state intervention; but in practice the same issues which gave rise to the quango phenomenon are now being handled by new instruments of public–private partnership, such as the arrangements described in this book. The likely shift from the centralized model of the MSC/Training Commission to a series of regional and local delivery agencies, in which industry (and any trades unions which care to be involved) is responsible for the delivery of major public programmes, is hardly a rejection of indirect administration. Indeed, it may perhaps be a new form of neo-corporatism. Concepts such as 'leverage' and public 'pump-priming' have become more acceptable than new quangos (even though some of those have been produced – such as Urban Development Corporations) as an ideologically acceptable form of public–private interdependency in meeting the government's policy or objectives. When, as we argued in Chapter 1, the government has to be seen to act (and to spend), acceptable means have to be found for delivering the necessary funds and action. *In principle*, much of what has been done in response to the unemployment crisis could have been delivered by existing institutional structures – particularly by regional and local authorities – with direct funding from national government. That this form of delivery has not been chosen is possibly a reflection of the government's own disenchantment with the capacity of *existing* institutions to 'deliver' effectively and a reflection of the need to maintain the 'tough' image of strict controls on expenditure, particularly by local authorities. Somehow, the need to be seen to act had to be fitted in with certain self-imposed restraints on the government of the day.

These practical and political considerations are, however, underpinned by a more coherent philosophical or theoretical view. For example, some writers on public-private interaction view the development of corporate responsibility in meeting social objectives as increasingly important and indeed desirable. Kempner, Macmillan and Hawkins (1974) describe a 'paradigm shift' in the mode of interaction between the business corporation and society. The competitive liberal economic tradition which identified the pursuit of corporate profit maximization with the interests of the wider community, as mediated through the market, has become increasingly at variance with the reality of economic organizations and structures based on collectivism and professional management. More particularly, changes in social values have placed less emphasis on competition, economic self-interest and profit as indicators of progress, and more on collective community welfare. These shifts, it is argued, will lead to increasing pressure on the traditions of corporate enterprise, but as yet the reorientation of business objectives and values to fit the new social aspirations has lacked an appropriate theory to guide managers.

Kempner, Macmillan and Hawkins (1974), argue the need for a new social consensus which will integrate private action and public goods, without centralizing social decision-making. They talk of a fusion of consensus and competition which will preserve the basic values of a pluralist liberal society, although they do not specify in any detail how this fusion might be achieved. Beesley and Evans also analyse this problem of coping with social change while preserving the framework of social stability and liberal pluralism, echoing Smith's (1975) call for the new partnership institutions or societal administration to generate public confidence in order to avoid 'drastic swings in policy and eruption of destructive ideological conflicts' (Beesley and Evans, 1978).

Here we begin to see hints of a deeper motivation for the development of partnership schemes such as LEAs – namely, that much of this activity can be understood only in the context of *system-maintaining* behaviour. It is perhaps no accident that many of those involved in the early stages of the development of the corporate responsibility movement in Britain were attracted to the idea in response to urban riots, which they saw as early signs that society might be destabilized (Richardson, 1983). Action to dampen down a burgeoning sense of grievance was consistent both with perfectly genuine personal concern for the welfare of the disadvantaged in society *and* with a desire to maintain the existing 'order' of things. Beesley and Evans (1978) argue that there are limits to the capacity of the market system and the 'public choice system' (by which they mean the political process) to regulate and handle emerging social needs. This suggests that a third system, which has been relegated to a lesser role in the past, will become increasingly significant in the future. They call this system 'societal self-regulation' and see corporate responsibility as one major component of this third way. It would require changes of attitude not only within management but also in government, with new organizational networks emerging based on mutual dependency and dual legitimacy. For the corporation, social responsibility becomes an issue of how far it is able to incorporate external concerns into its own decision-making process and to participate in creating new organizational coalitions or co-operative institutions.

Given these general pressures on the role of the corporation in society, how can we characterize the response of business? We might well expect variations in corporate philosophy on social responsibility. For example, Grant, in an analysis of the political strategies of British business, identified three basic orientations towards political involvement and lobbying: the *tripartite* firm, which is active in associational networks and recognizes government intervention as reasonable in certain circumstances; the *capitalist aggressive* firm, which regards close relations with government as a constraint on operational efficiency and sees its societal relations as being essentially defined by the market (and is therefore not active in business groups); and the *pragmatic* firm, which lacks a corporate political philosophy but reacts to the immediate environment in order to protect its interests (Grant, 1987).

Beesley and Evans (1978) also conceive of a spectrum of corporate social involvement but along two variables:

(1) *internalization* – the extent to which the corporation incorporates external issues into its own structures and processes;

(2)   *external relationships* – the degree of responsiveness to the outside world.

At one end of the spectrum are companies characterized by 'passive adaptation', responding simply to the demands of the law, political force, or social custom, and where there is no engagement in external negotiation to change these parameters. For example, in a case study of corporate responsibility in UK firms, Harvey, Smith and Wilkinson (1984) saw this kind of response as one where companies regarded the outside world 'like the weather' – something that one had to react to, but could do nothing to change. The mid-point in Beesley and Evans's spectrum involved companies showing an awareness of external concerns and a commitment to legitimize corporate activities in relation to these concerns. This approach is still a highly reactive response, but can lead on to a stage where companies begin to negotiate and bargain with their environment rather than simply internalize concerns without trying to influence them. At the final point of the spectrum, firms engage in external negotiation and also internal adaptation, incorporating external concerns into their own decision-making system. Here the corporation actively searches for appropriate responses and does not view outside forces simply as operational constraints. Our review of local partnerships as a response to unemployment has illustrated that British business is *somewhere* on this continuum and that there is some evidence that it is moving towards the more sophisticated responses which might be classed as 'external negotiation' in some cases. If this is the case, then there may be some important implications for the future organization of society's response to critical issues.

The implications of public policy partnership

It would be misleading to view the LEA type of partnership as simply another variant of 'privatization', although it may contain elements of this. It is more about mobilizing private-sector resources to perform tasks or solve public policy issues. Critically, the impact of enterprise trusts as agents of economic change is based on a mix of public and private resources, not on the replacement of one by the other. (Indeed, the mix of resources is still weighted in favour of the public sector.) Certainly, the peer-group pressure on firms to participate in enterprise trusts seems far removed from any notions of privatization. The image is more of business leaders being sucked into helping solve public policy problems, and of a government keen to spread responsibility, than of any straightforward notion of privatization. Thus, the process consists as much of 'contracting in' as of the 'contracting out' which is normally associated with privatization – even if exactly what everyone is contracting into is not clear. Both local government, voluntary organizations and business may have drifted into the new partnership arrangements without fully realizing what was going on or how it might change their respective roles and responsibilities in the long run. Perhaps only central government has had a reasonably clear notion of what it intended to achieve by encouraging and funding these changes. With hindsight, it seems that the sum total of governmental actions may reflect a pattern – the outflanking of some existing institutions and the weakening of certain established interests.

From the perspective of business, the normative values accepted by most British business leaders, and referred to earlier, are important in understanding how this 'contracting in' can be achieved. In the UK there has been a general societal acceptance of state intervention, especially in social policy. As Harvey, Smith and Wilkinson (1984) argue, post-Victorian business interests recognized that corporate paternalism was inadequate to cope with the rising social needs and legacy of industrialism, and that the costs of provision should not be carried by individual enterprises but collectively through state welfare. Not only was this seen as a more effective and efficient means of attaining social welfare goals, but it could service the interests of business by producing a better-educated or healthier workforce. At the same time, the advance of welfarism reflected the pressures of organized labour and provided a means of accommodating this interest within the capitalist system. Similarly, UK urban policy has hitherto been dominated by the ideology of public intervention and public investment designed to facilitate private growth or to mitigate the adverse impacts of industrialism. This fits in well with the social welfare tradition of British capitalism. The 1977 White Paper on urban policy emphasized the importance of private investment and economic development in the inner cities, but also saw local authorities as the 'natural agencies' for renewal (Department of the Environment, 1977). Local government was given enhanced powers, and the inner-city partnerships were established as *partnerships between different tiers of the public sector.*

Thus, British business leaders have long been used to close state involvement in society and have often seen state intervention as central in furthering the long-term interests of capital (Vogel, 1986). Having become familiar with, and to some degree relaxed about, state involvement, it was not difficult for senior business leaders to accept a closer working relationship with the state, following a change in urban policy post-1979. Now the whole concept of urban partnership has changed to one based on public–private interaction at a policy-formulation and project-implementation level. As the CBI itself has argued: 'urban areas will only be regenerated if both private and public sectors work together in partnership' (CBI, 1986, p. 8). More recently, the CBI has published the report of its Task Force on Business and Urban Regeneration. Again the partnership between the public and private sectors is emphasized, as is the key role of business leaders 'in providing the necessary enterprise, energy, and credibility to attract private sector investors on the scale required' (CBI, 1988).

This is not to suggest, however, that business leaders are unaware of the costs of being 'contracted in'. The Conservative government's plans, announced in 1986, to develop up to twenty City Technology Colleges, free from local authority control and financed in part by industry, ran into difficulties when it emerged that business leaders were reluctant to accept this new responsibility. Though some companies agreed to participate and provide funds, many of the large corporations – such as Imperial Chemical Industries – declined to be involved. The colleges, for 11–18-year-olds, will receive government funding equivalent to existing local authority expenditure, but industry is expected to find most of the capital funding. Having invested a significant amount of political capital in this policy idea, the government had to set up a special charitable trust to act as an umbrella organization for the initiative as it ran into difficulties in the spring of 1987. Seemingly, business leaders had recognized that being asked to provide capital funding for schools was pressing the developing sense of corporate responsibility a little too far too fast. In the event, the government is having to find large sums of money itself, in order to keep the initiative alive.

The impact of developing corporate responsibility

Evaluating the significance of local initiatives and the increasingly high public profile of corporate responsibility in the UK involves two levels of analysis. First, the explicit, publicly stated aims of corporate involvement are to achieve desirable socioeconomic goals, including employment, urban renewal and new enterprise formation. It is this level which has occupied most of this book. However, behind this lies a second level of analysis, involving implicit political and ideological objectives which are significant but subject to far less critical scrutiny.

If one looks at the more overt public objectives, we have already argued that the actual measurable effects of corporate responsibility in the UK are probably relatively small. Only a few major companies make a sophisticated and systematic institutionalized response to the unemployment issue in terms of developing policy strategies and an organizational commitment. Even in these cases, it is important to place the level of this activity in perspective. In terms of bending corporate resources to support public policy goals in the field of unemployment, the commitment is valuable, but it is ultimately marginal and is often offset by the continued process of corporate rationalization and restructuring which reduces employment opportunities. Indeed, corporate restructuring is often the critical factor in influencing companies to become involved in local initiatives in response to local pressures and in order to preserve local legitimacy.

For example, Pilkington in St Helens has reduced its local workforce from a peak of 20,000 to a current level of 7,000 and over the last decade has halved its local workforce. It was this scale of rationalization and the dominance of Pilkington as an employer and local social institution which generated the company response to local economic decline through co-sponsorship of the first enterprise trust in the UK, the Community of St Helens Trust, in 1977. The agency costs approximately £100,000 per annum to run, of which it is estimated that Pilkington meets 40 per cent (Fazey, 1987). In addition, the company has supported other economic development initiatives, including a venture capital fund. Against these commitments, the company has spent some £90 million on cumulative redundancy payments (Fazey, 1987). The process of corporate rationalization has helped transform the trading position of the company. After recovering from the costs of provision for redundancies and poor trading performances, Pilkington announced record pre-tax profits of £256 million in 1986 (see the *Guardian*, 11 June 1987). Profits rose to £302 million in the following year, on worldwide sales of £2.3 billion.

The difficulty in reconciling the internal needs of the corporation with its broader social responsibilities was particularly evident in the autumn of 1988, when Pilkington had to decide on the UK location of its new £65 million plant. The Chief Executive of Pilkington Glass

Ltd had recommended that the new plant should be located in Kent, close to the South-East of England with its more favourable growth in demand. The recommendation provoked a joint campaign by local councillors and trades union leaders designed to persuade the company to locate the new plant in St Helens. Councillor Mike Doyle, the Chairman of the Economic Development Committee in St Helens, is quoted as saying that 'At a time when we are rebuilding the town, Pilkington's decision to go south could be perceived as a major company running away. Something like this could have a very detrimental effect, and we don't want to take that gamble' (*Financial Times*, 18 October 1988). In the event, Pilkington decided on St Helens, rather than Kent, on commercial grounds, although the Chairman of the company commented: 'I don't accept that we owe St Helens any form of debt'.

All this is not to dismiss Pilkington's contribution to alleviating the unemployment crisis in St Helens as either symbolic or uncaring, but simply to place that response in its wider context of corporate decision-making. It is not inconsistent to argue that Pilkington has contributed significantly in terms of UK corporate responsibility, while at the same time suggesting that, at least in the short to medium terms, the impact on the local community may be relatively marginal as the company believes that it has to rationalize in order to stay competitive. This is a perfectly respectable argument within the framework of a competitive privately owned economy. Had Pilkington *not* rationalized and reduced its workforce, even *more* jobs would in all probability have been lost. Many large firms – widely recognized as good employers – had to face this dilemma as Britain finally tried to achieve the productivity levels of its competitors in the 1980s. Slimming down was essential to the survival of the business itself (and hence to the survival of at least *some* employment), and companies had no choice but to 'rationalize'. That this process coincided with a greater sense of community involvement, particularly in the form of participation in LEAs, was perhaps a necessary irony. The point we make is not one of criticism of corporate responses – far from it, we applaud them – but one of scale. Thus, we need to set against this important phenomenon the scale of the business concerned.

Two further illustrations will suffice to make this general point. In 1983–4 British Petroleum spent £2.5 million under its community affairs budget. In 1983 the Group's profits were £866 million. As reported in the *Financial Times* (22 July 1986), Marks & Spencer will spend £1.5 billion in the period 1986–90 building new stores, compared with a social responsibility budget of between £2 million and £3 million over the same period. These cases are cited not to criticize the adequacy or otherwise of individual company responses. Indeed, we recognize that it is extremely difficult to measure the extent of company effort, because so much of it is through seconding staff. Thus, purely financial measures are likely to underestimate company involvement. The companies mentioned can be considered to be at the forefront of UK corporate responsibility. It is important, however, to place corporate commitment in some kind of context. The companies involved would not claim that their activities are the solution to the problem of local unemployment, only part of a wider response in partnership with public agencies. The contributions are undoubtedly seen as significant by the companies concerned, and it can be argued that they do make a useful input to the search for more effective policy responses or programme delivery at local levels, without really impinging on the strategic decisions of companies in areas like purchasing and contracting, employment and training, or the development of new products.

The politics of corporate responsibility

Economic explanations for what is happening are only partial explanations. One must also seek to understand the *politics of private-sector involvement in public issues such as unemployment.* This leads us to further consider the underlying motivation for this phenomenon, and at this level of analysis we can observe two fundamental theoretical perspectives.

The dominant analytical perspective on corporate responsibility is locked into certain basic assumptions about society. These assumptions can be broadly characterized as based on liberal democratic political theory, emphasizing in particular pluralism, where the corporation is seen as one among a galaxy of social institutions influencing the political process. The issue of corporate management becomes one of how to respond to this 'negotiated environment' (Thomas, 1976) both as an issue of functional necessity and to preserve the legitimacy of the corporation within the social system. Writers on corporate responsibility have been influenced by managerialist theories which argue that the separation of ownership and control in the modern corporation is a potentially important force in extending managerial autonomy and the capacity of the organization to take a wider view of its responsibilities within society (Nicols, 1969).

Unlike economic liberals, these writers recognize that simply looking to the market as a mechanism for structuring the relationship between the corporation and society is inadequate, given the complex interaction of social forces generated by the growth of government, the emergence of new pressure groups and the changing structure of business itself. The function of the corporation is still primarily an economic one, based on the market, but this inevitably leads to a host of 'secondary' relationships and impacts which cannot be handled through the market (Preston and Post, 1975).

The literature of this dominant perspective then sets out to examine the responsiveness of the corporation to its socioeconomic environment. Some writers may explicitly recognize the broader ideological motives behind this responsiveness. For example, Preston has observed: 'The great bulk of corporate philanthropic activities has no connection whatsoever with profit seeking behaviour or any other conventional business management goal. It does, however, have a great deal to do with the preservation of the social system within which the corporation operates' (Preston, 1986, p. 215). On the other hand, the response of corporations can be divorced seemingly, from any ideological context and reduced to the level of technical organizational analysis. For example, Ackerman argues: 'the problems posed by society's quest for socially responsive corporations are most usefully interpreted as managerial in nature rather than ethical or ideological' (Ackerman, 1975, p. 1).

Writers from this liberal managerialist school of analysis can become highly prescriptive, urging corporations to respond to environmental pressures in order to preserve the pluralistic liberal social system or more basically to preserve the legitimacy of the corporation (Kempner, Macmillan and Hawkins, 1974; Beesley and Evans, 1978). Both the more philosophical liberal-values approach and the managerialist functionalist school (Clutterbuck, 1981) of corporate responsibility share a common belief in the liberal democratic political system and the 'mixed' capitalist economy. For example, in outlining its new approach to the inner cities' problems, BIC has argued that the private sector has to recognize not only the incentives to be involved, but also the high price of neglect in terms of social breakdown or withdrawal of social consent (BIC, 1986, p. 10). Similarly, the CBI's Task Force on Business and Urban Regeneration, cited earlier, has emphasized the costs to business of urban decay – such as less spending by city residents, wasted land development opportunities, problems in recruiting young people and increasing skill shortages.

The concern with preserving established social structures, and ensuring the continuation of corporate legitimacy and managerial autonomy, is clearly apparent in the public pronouncements made by the leaders of British industry in explaining the need for companies to become more socially responsible and responsive. The driving force behind BIC reflects the conception of 'enlightened self-interest' expressed by Lord Carr and referred to earlier. This may involve specific participation in emerging public policies like the Youth Training Scheme, to render these more 'relevant' to industry's needs. For example, the CBI's Special Programme Unit proclaimed that active involvement by companies in the YTS would: 'Help to produce a government policy that is founded on the realities of the mid-1980s workplace and make sure that it will facilitate what we believe will be the position towards the end of the century' (CBI, 1983).

Useem has introduced the notion of 'classwide benefits' to explain corporate social activity. Thus, he argues:

> A new conception of the business firm is also needed. Most corporate business discussions are viewed, correctly, as a product of the internal logic of the firm. Yet when decisions are made on the allocation of monies to political candidates, the direction of philanthropic activities and other forms of political outreach, an external logic is important as well. *This is the logic of classwide benefits, involving considerations that lead to company decisions beneficial to all large companies, even when there is no discernible, direct gain for the individual firm.*
>
> (Useem, 1984, p. 5, our emphasis)

There is also a strong belief emerging that the private sector must become involved in issues such as unemployment and urban unrest, because the consequences of 'doing nothing' are too dangerous. For instance, it may be that the government increasingly feels impelled to intervene directly in the economy in ways which run counter to the business community's perception of its own interests:

> companies fear that if they make no attempt to find solutions to community problems the government may increasingly take on the responsibility itself. This might prove costly both in terms of

new obligations and greater intervention in the labour market. Many companies prefer to be one step ahead of government legislation or intervention, to anticipate social pressure themselves, and hence be able to develop their own policies in response to them.

(CBI, 1982)

Ultimately, the future of the private enterprise system may be undermined. As Lord Seiff, Chairman of Marks & Spencer, one of the leading exponents of corporate social responsibility in Britain, has argued:

If we who manage do not appreciate the value of, and pursue in this day and age with patience and tenacity, a policy of good human relations and constructive involvement in the community, then we must not be surprised if we wake up one morning to find ourselves members of a society that few of us want, where democratic values no longer operate and there is little freedom. Then we should only have ourselves to blame.'

(BIC, n.d.)

Alternative class-based radical theories of society would criticize these functionalist and pluralist models, focusing instead on concentrations of economic and political power and on contradictory class interests. On this view of society, organizations reflect the wider class-based society, and fundamentally the role of corporate social responsibility operates within the constraints of capital (Burrell and Morgan, 1979). From this radically different perspective, which emphasizes conflicts within the social system and competing ideological interests, the corporation is regarded as an agency of capital in the development of strategies to control and shape the environment. Corporate social responsibility might then be seen as a new element in the strategy of control which aims to manage new socioeconomic conflicts, such as urban riots and rising unemployment, in order to preserve an economic system based on private enterprise.

Whether pluralist/consensus theories or more radical theories provide a more rigorous explanation of increased private-sector involvement in the shape of the corporate responsibility movement, the fact is that big business has accepted the need for, and has adapted to, the role of the state in economic planning and in welfare provision, and is also increasingly recognizing, at least at peak levels of business leadership, that corporations must play a more proactive role in managing social problems. The issues of unemployment and urban decay are among the biggest issues facing public policy. We have pointed to the relatively successful *political* management of the unemployment issue by the Conservative governments since 1979 (Moon and Richardson, 1984). A key political response has been to place faith in the role of the private sector in helping to resolve this social problem. This underlines the view of Harvey, Smith and Wilkinson that: 'The role in society of business, that is the operation of privately owned firms, or what is often called free enterprise, is a broadly political-ideological issue' (1984, p. 2).

Current government thinking on the role of private enterprise and corporate responsibility combines technical and ideological assumptions. The technical assumptions concern the respective capacities of the public and private sectors to resolve social issues. There is a recognition of the practical limits on what government can achieve, although where these 'limits' are actually set is also a political and ideological issue. The search for new public-private relationships and for new institutions of policy delivery is presented as a technical search compatible with the values of liberal pluralism.

In practical terms, corporate involvement in anti-unemployment schemes and in inner-city renewal projects is perhaps a political alternative to more collectivist strategies favoured by the left. The emergence of the inner cities problem as perhaps *the* most central issue after the 1987 general election served to emphasize the Conservative government's more general commitment to partnership between the public and private sectors as a solution to societal problems such as unemployment, arts sponsorship and educational reform. No doubt books are now being written on 'partnership in response to urban decay', since this policy area also exhibits exactly the same phenomenon.

Finally, there has been a political and ideological concern with the need to stimulate and preserve an 'entrepreneurial culture'. The present government obviously has an ideological commitment to this, but the emphasis on developing small businesses and providing public money to encourage almost any entrepreneurial activity is supported by virtually all political parties. In so far as big business participates in the setting up of, say, enterprise trusts, it is helping to reinforce society's commitment to entrepreneurship as a solution to our problems. As Useem suggests, corporate responsibility programmes 'help shape the national political culture, the ideas and leaders that prosper, the ideologies and candidates that fail' (Useem, 1984, p. 116). That local authorities have been very willing participants in this process is indicative of the shift in cultural values which appears to be taking place. Such shifts in values are difficult to detect at the time, and present trends may yet be reversed. Our guess is that the real effects of the type of partnership scheme which we have examined are in terms not of jobs created or jobs saved, or of the number of firms created or the growth in firms, but of the social and political management of a stressful problem and of the creation of a new spirit of entrepreneurship and self-help.

In the longer term, the economic impacts may be important. In the medium term, it is the changes in culture, ideas and the balance of political power between public and private sectors and between central and local government which are significant. In the short term, these initiatives represent a symbol and/or pragmatic response to a major social, economic and political problem – namely, unemployment. Undoubtedly, the partnership movement is increasingly business orientated, in the context of a central governmental concern to re-establish and extend a dynamic capitalist economy. Whether or not one supports this underlying political objective depends in the last analysis on where one stands in the political spectrum. As co-authors of this book, we might have differing political perspectives, but to ignore this aspect of the partnership movement would be to miss a central element in its dynamic.

Note

An earlier version of most of this chapter appeared in *Research in Corporate Social Performance and Policy*, vol. 10, pp. 267–91, 1988.

References

Ackerman, R. W. (1975), *The Social Challenge to Business* (Cambridge, Mass.: Harvard University Press).

Antal, A. B. (1985), 'Institutionalizing corporate social responsiveness: lessons learned from the MIGROS experience', *Research in Corporate Social Performance and Policy*, vol. 7, pp. 229–49.

Beesley, M. and Evans, T. (1978), *Corporate Social Responsibility* (London: Croom Helm).

Burrell, G. and Morgan, G. (1979), *Sociological Paradigms and Organizational Analysis* (London: Heinemann Educational), especially Part II.

Business in the Community (1986), *Newsletter*, summer.

BIC (n.d.), *A Guide to Action* (London: BIC).

Confederation of British Industry (1982), *Company Responses to Unemployment* (London: CBI).

CBI (1983), *Community Action Programmes 1981–3*, report by Special Programmes Unit (London: CBI).

CBI (1986), *Reviving the Cities* (London: CBI).

CBI (1988), *Initiatives Beyond Charity*, report by CBI Task Force on Business and Urban Regeneration (London: CBI).

Chandler, J. A. and Lawless, P. (1985), *Local Authorities and the Creation of Employment* (Aldershot: Gower).

Clutterbuck, D. (1981), *How To Be a Good Corporate Citizen: A Manager's Guide to Making Social Responsibility Work and Pay* (Maidenhead: McGraw-Hill).

Department of the Environment (1977), *Policy for the Inner Cities*, Cmnd 6845 (London: HMSO).

Drucker, P. (1984), 'Converting social problems into business opportunities: the new meaning of corporate social responsibility', *California Management Review*, vol. XXVI, no. 2, winter, pp. 53–63.

Fazey, I. H. (1987), *The Pathfinders* (London: Financial Training Publications).

Grant, W. (1987), *Business and Politics in Britain* (Basingstoke: Macmillan Education).

Harvey, B., Smith, S., and Wilkinson, B. (1984), *Managers and Corporate Social Policy: Private Solutions to Public Problems?* (London: Macmillan).

Kempner, T., Macmillan, K., and Hawkins, K. (1974), *Business and Society: Transition and Change* (London: Allen Lane).

McArthur, A. A., and McGregor, A. (1987), 'Local employment and training initiatives in the national manpower policy context', in V. Hausner (ed.), *Critical Issues in Urban Economic Development*, Vol. II (Oxford: Oxford University Press), pp. 116–59.

Mawson, J., and Miller, D. (1987), 'Interventionist approaches in local employment and economic development: the experience of Labour local authorities', in V. Hausner (ed.) (1987), *Critical Issues in Urban Economic Development*, vol. II (Oxford: Oxford University Press).

Moon, J., and Richardson, J. J. (1984), *Unemployment in the UK: Politics and Policies* (Aldershot: Gower).

Moore, C., and Richardson, J. J. (1988), 'The politics and practice of corporate responsibility in Great Britain', in L. Preston (ed.) *Research in Corporate Social Performance and Policy*, Volume 10 (Greenwich, Conn: JAI).

Nicos, T. (1969), *Ownership, Control and Democracy: An Enquiry into Certain Aspects of Modern Business Ideology* (London: Allen & Unwin).

Preston, L. E. (1986), *Social Issues and Public Policy in Business and Management. Retrospect and Prospect* (Maryland: Center for Business and Public Policy, University of Maryland).

Preston, L. E., and Post, J. E. (1975), *Private Management and Public Policy: The Principle of Public Responsibility* (Englewood Cliffs, NJ: Prentice-Hall).

Rein, M. (1982), 'The social policy of the firm', *Policy Sciences*, vol. 14, no. 2, April, pp. 117–35.

Rhodes, R. A. W. (1988), *Beyond Westminster and Whitehall: The Sub-Central Governments of Britain* (London: Unwin Hyman).

Richardson, J. J. (1983), *The Development of Corporate Responsibility in the UK*, Strathclyde Papers on Government and Politics, No. 1 (Glasgow: Department of Politics, University of Strathclyde).

Richardson, J. J. (1988), 'Britain: changing policy styles and policy innovation in response to economic crisis', in E. Damgaard, P. Gerlich and J. J. Richardson, *The Politics of Economic Crisis: Lessons from Western Europe* (Aldershot: Gower), pp. 8–28.

Smith, B. L. R. (1975), 'The public use of the private sector', in B. Smith (ed.), *The New Political Economy: The Public Use of the Private Sector* (London: Macmillan), pp. 1–45.

Thomas, R. E. (1976), *The Government of Business* (Oxford: Philip Allan).

Useem, M. (1984), *The Inner Circle: Large Corporations and the Rise of Business Political Activity in the US and UK* (New York: Oxford University Press).

Vogel, D. (1986), *National Styles of Regulation: Environmental Policy in Great Britain and the United States* (Ithaca, NY, and London: Cornell University Press).

Wolman, H. (1987), 'Urban economic performance: a comparative analysis', in V. Hausner (ed.), *Critical Issues in Urban Economic Development*, Vol. II (Oxford: Oxford University Press), pp. 9–43.

Index

Printed in the United States
by Baker & Taylor Publisher Services